ACKNOWLEDGMENTS

Many minds and hands worked together in the production of this report. A few of those whom we owe a debt of gratitude included Austin Institute Senior Fellow Professor Mark Regnerus, Betsy Stokes for her careful editing, Nicholas McCann and Andrea Dahm for art direction and graphic design, Dr. Bill Taylor, Miguel Gabian, and María José Ruiz Gonzalez for additional editing support. Finally, translation services provided by Ms. Consuelo Rueda and Ms. Irene Escobar. We must thank them especially for the difficult work of breaking down language barriers in social science.

TABLE OF CONTENTS

INTRODUCTION 1
LATINO DEMOGRAPHICS 2
LATINOS & VOTING 4
LATINOS & THE CONSTITUTION 8
LATINO CIVIC KNOWLEDGE 10
LATINO ECONOMIC VIEWS 12
LATINOS & RELIGION 15
LATINO FAMILIES 21
LATINO MARRIAGE & FAMILIES 24
LATINOS & ABORTION 36
CONCLUSION 38
REFERENCES 39
ENDNOTES 42
APPENDIX 46

INTRODUCTION

Reminiscent of Herbert Hoover's promise of "a chicken in every pot," there is now "a Latino in every home," quips Latino comedian George Lopez, "whether you live there, or you work there." Then he becomes more poignant: "So [Latino women] raise their kids and they raise other kids. Little white kids that are gonna understand Latinos, because they're gonna have brown hearts."[1]

Is America developing a brown heart? This is precisely the hope or fear or perplexity experienced by so many Americans today.

From the historical surges of Irish, Italians, Chinese, and Eastern Europeans, to the more recent waves of immigrants from parts of Latin America and Africa, to the present-day debates about welcoming or rejecting refugees from the Middle East, the process of immigration to the United States rarely comes without dispute and conflict. Competition for jobs, the costs of educating and socially supporting new arrivals (including incarcerating and litigating the undocumented), the safety of citizens, and the decline of English as the common language are just a few of the issues that fuel heated debates over immigration policy. Protesters of strict immigration laws insist, "No human being is illegal!" while Republican presidential candidate Donald Trump aimed to secure votes by a policy of mass Latin American deportation and "a big, beautiful, powerful wall" featuring a strictly monitored "gate."[2]

Many are asking, where do the millions of Latino immigrants fit within the American mosaic? Unfortunately, the lives of Latinos in America are often discussed in anecdotal terms, with little factual information or helpful insight. To find out what their lives are like, we have to ask them. That's why this report draws from one of the largest representative samples of this growing population, the *Relationships in America Survey* (RIA). We study data from this survey to seek to understand the beliefs, experiences, and lifestyle choices that truly characterize Latinos in America. The quality and richness of the survey data allow for an evidence-based approach that moves beyond the caricatures to honestly enlighten while opening up avenues of future discussion and debate.

Commissioned by the Austin Institute for the Study of Family and Culture, the RIA examined the family composition, beliefs, experiences, and behaviors reported by U.S. residents in January and February 2014. The target population was noninstitutionalized[3] adults aged 18–60, and 15,738 surveys were completed (62 percent). Surveys were conducted in English or Spanish, based on the respondent's preference. In the RIA, we often sort respondents by race/ethnicity in order to offer comparisons of their views, and we focus in particular on the experiences of Latinos. The goal is to discover their core beliefs, their lived experiences, and the facts about their makeup as a group.

First, using data from the much larger 2010 U.S. Census report,[4] we present a brief demographic profile of U.S. Latinos. We then move to using our more recent data to consider their political attitudes. The RIA survey asked questions about voter preference, satisfaction with the political system, and even basic knowledge of U.S. history and the Constitution. Then we turn to questions about economic issues, exploring whether respondents are more apt to agree with liberal or conservative fiscal policies.

We follow this with a discussion of religion and religious beliefs before concluding with an evaluation of family dynamics, practices, and attitudes. For this, we asked questions related to early life experiences and the quality of respondents' relationships with their parents during childhood and adolescence, as well as how Latinos view traditional family roles and the importance they attribute to key dimensions of family life. We also asked the hard political questions about abortion, same-sex marriage, and the definition of "family."

LATINO DEMOGRAPHICS

Latinos residing in the United States are a diverse group that includes persons of Mexican, Cuban, Puerto Rican, South American, Central American, and other Spanish-speaking origins. According to the 2010 Census, of the nearly 309 million people living in the United States, approximately 16 percent (or roughly 50 million) were of Latino origin. They might be American citizens (natural-born or naturalized) or citizens of their country of origin. They could be first-generation immigrants or might trace their U.S. residency back many generations. Although a common link among them is Spanish language and culture, some speak only Spanish, many are English-language learners or bilingual, and some predominantly speak English. The recent growth of the U.S. population as a whole—something characteristic of a vibrant society—is largely a result of the increasing Latino population over the past decade: between 2000 and 2010, the Latino population grew by 43 percent, which was four times the 10 percent overall growth in the total population.[5]

Furthermore, it is estimated that approximately 16 percent of U.S. Latinos are undocumented.[6] Although the possibility does exist that undocumented U.S. Latinos may have participated in our survey, it is more likely that they would have declined, for fear of discovery and deportation.

In the U.S., the majority of persons who self-identify as Latino are of Mexican origin.

In the United States, the majority of persons who self-identify as Latino are of Mexican origin (63 percent), followed by Puerto Ricans (9 percent) and Cubans (4 percent).

Over the past decade the Latino population grew at four times the rate of the total population.

LATINO DEMOGRAPHICS

Several noteworthy demographic characteristics about education and employment can help us to better understand this group:

- **Latino teenagers drop out of high school at a higher-than-average rate.** In 2010, the percentage of all Americans aged sixteen through nineteen who had dropped out of high school was approximately 6 percent. For non-Latino whites, it was 4 percent, and for Latinos, it was 9 percent.

- **Latinos finish college at less than half the rate of the general population.** Approximately 28 percent of all adult Americans (31 percent of non-Latino white adults) had earned a bachelor's degree in 2010. The percentage for Latinos was 13 percent.

- **Latino households earn less.** The median household income in 2013 for all races was around $52,000 (for non-Latino whites, $58,000). It was approximately $41,000 for Latinos.

- **Latino poverty is high but decreasing.** While the 2013 poverty rate for non-Latino whites was 9.6 percent, the Latino poverty rate was 23.5 percent. However, both the Latino poverty rate and the total number of Latinos in poverty had decreased from their 2012 levels.[8]

Figure 1
Percent Latino by State

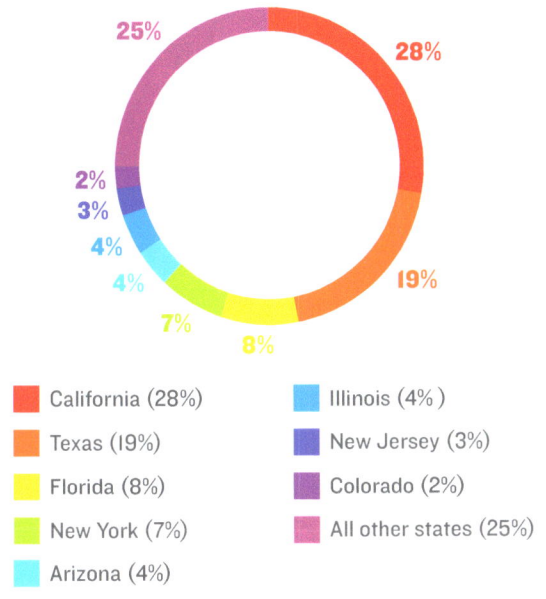

- California (28%)
- Texas (19%)
- Florida (8%)
- New York (7%)
- Arizona (4%)
- Illinois (4%)
- New Jersey (3%)
- Colorado (2%)
- All other states (25%)

Over half the Latino population in the U.S. resides in California, Texas, and Florida.

Adapted from: U.S. Census Bureau, 2010 Census Summary File 1.

Over half the Latino population in the United States resides in just three (big) states: California, Texas, and Florida (Figure 1). However, there has been recent and rapid growth of this group in other regions of the country, particularly in traditionally conservative "Bible Belt" states like Alabama, Mississippi, and South Carolina.[7]

LATINOS & VOTING

Patterns continue to indicate that only a minority of all eligible Americans show up to the polls during elections. These numbers tend to be even smaller among racial minorities and among Americans of lower socioeconomic status. We asked respondents if they would definitely be voting in the next presidential election (that is, 2016), if they thought they might vote, or if they intend to skip it.

Figure 2 displays voter intention by race/ethnicity. Latino Americans are the least likely to report that they "definitely" intend to vote. (Some, of course, are not eligible.) Whites are most likely, followed by African Americans. Twenty-nine percent of Latino respondents said they will likely not vote in the 2016 presidential election, a figure well above that of African Americans and whites. But we also see that Latinos have the highest percentage of uncertainty ("might vote")—one in four might vote—which speaks to potential for an increase in voter participation.

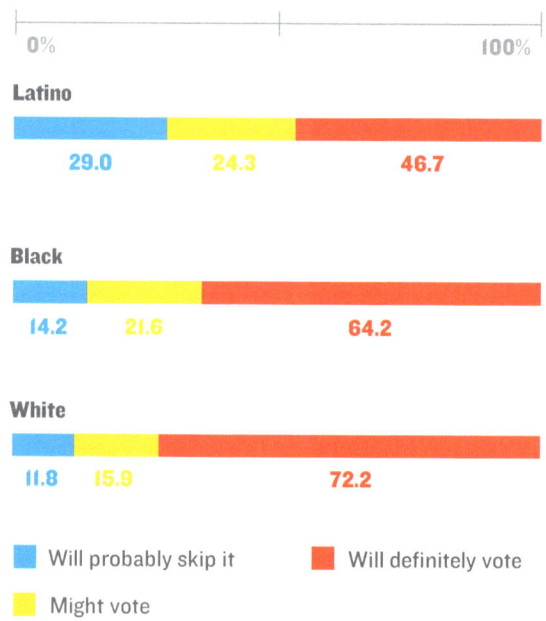

Figure 2
Likelihood of Voting in 2016, by Race/Ethnicity

Latino: 29.0 | 24.3 | 46.7

Black: 14.2 | 21.6 | 64.2

White: 11.8 | 15.9 | 72.2

■ Will probably skip it   ■ Will definitely vote
■ Might vote

Next we looked at voter intentions by a respondent's generational group (results not shown). We classified three groups: Millennials (ages 18–34), Generation Xers (ages 35–49) and Baby Boomers (those over 50). Older people were more likely to vote. Boomers reported the highest percentage of those definitely voting (78 percent), followed by GenXers (68 percent) and Millennials (54 percent). Conversely, Millennials are also the most likely to intend not to vote, as well as the most likely to report uncertainty about voting. Again, as with Latinos in general, this may indicate a potential voting bloc that is "up for grabs" if political parties can provide the motivation for these younger Americans to vote.

Figure 3
Likelihood of Voting in 2016, by Age Cohort (Latino only)

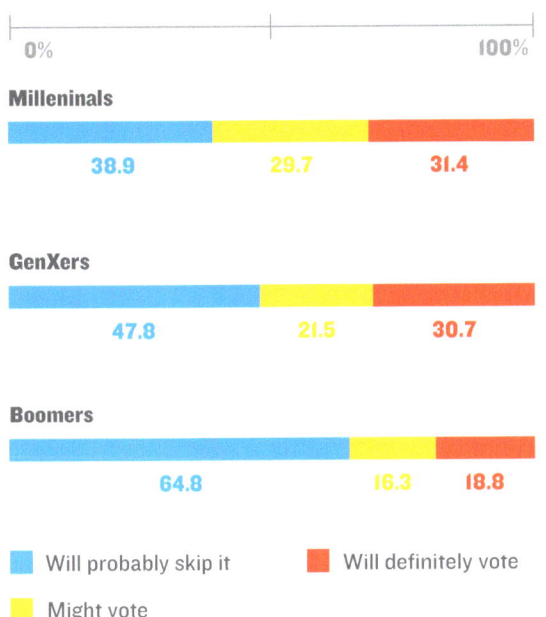

Figure 3 displays voter intention by generation, but exclusively for Latinos. The same age effect in the general population still stands—older Latinos are more likely to vote than younger ones. But even older Latinos are less apt to vote than are their counterparts in the general population, which is consistent with their diminished eligibility to do so. Sixty-five (65) percent of Latino Boomers report that they will definitely vote, compared to 78 percent of Boomers in general. (Both, historically, are overestimates of actual voting patterns.) Latino GenXers and Millennials plan to turn out in comparably low numbers compared to their peers in the country at large. Just as in the general population, Latino Millennials are the age group most likely not to vote in the presidential election, though Latino GenXers are close behind. Campaigns, then, target no more than half, and quite possibly well under half, of young Latino Americans. The rest either are ineligible to vote or are electing to opt out.

It's Latinos who are more likely than others to fly the liberal flag.

What are the political orientations of Latinos in America? Most of us presume they lean liberal. Is that the case? Respondents were asked whether they consider themselves very conservative, conservative, middle-of-the-road, liberal, or very liberal. Figure 4a documents that the distribution of political orientations seems quite similar across racial and ethnic groups, swelling in the middle and thinning out at the extremes. Whites are most likely to call themselves conservative, and Blacks least likely, which is old news to pollsters. However, as a larger percentage of Black respondents identify as middle-of-the-road when compared to whites and Latinos, it's Latinos who are more likely than others to fly the liberal flag. Nearly 28 percent identify as being liberal or very liberal, in comparison to about 21 percent of whites and 25 percent of African Americans.

Figure 4b again displays political orientation across generation, but this time just for Latinos. Again, increases in age are associated with political conservatism. But overall, Latinos are more liberal than the population as a whole. Only 35 percent of Latino Boomers report being politically conservative (to any degree), where they are joined by 32 percent of Latino GenXers and just 23 percent of Latino Millennials.

The next set of figures shows us how likely respondents said they would be to vote for a Republican candidate in the 2016 presidential election. The survey was administered before any candidate had declared their intention to pursue the presidency, so our question is limited to party preference rather than about particular candidates.

While no shortage of Americans call themselves conservative, asking them about voting Republican reveals that when the rubber meets the road plenty of "conservatives" were not intending to vote for the GOP in 2016. Interestingly, as with voter turnout, Latinos were most likely to give a neutral answer, indicating once again they were the least decided. White Americans unsurprisingly considered themselves most apt to support a GOP candidate in the 2016 presidential election (at 53 percent: 30 percent "very likely" and 23 percent "somewhat likely"). Comparable numbers for Blacks and Latinos were only 15 and 41 percent, respectively. Whereas African Americans remain steady supporters of Democratic candidates, at least when it comes to presidential races, the 41 percent of Latino voters reflects patterns more similar to white voters than Black ones. This suggests that both political parties have issues on which they might be successful in aligning Latinos with their respective messages. Moreover, these results suggest that racial minorities may not be as monolithic a voting bloc for the Democratic Party as is often suggested in popular media.

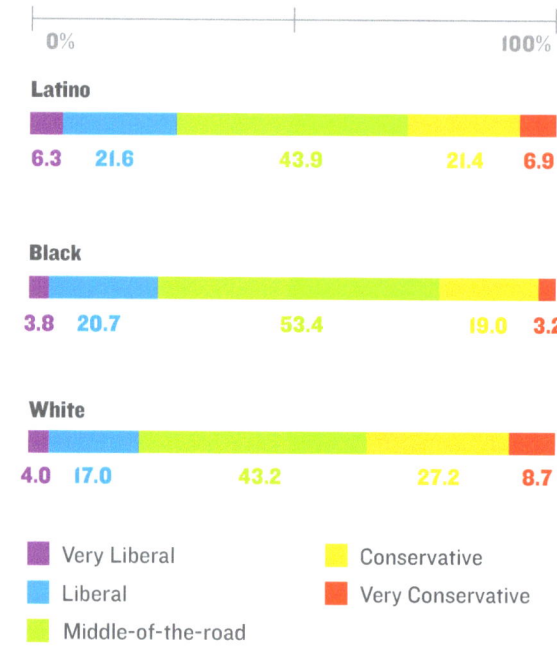

Figure 4a
Political Orientation, by Race/Ethnicity

Figure 4b
Political Orientation, by Age Cohort (Latino only)

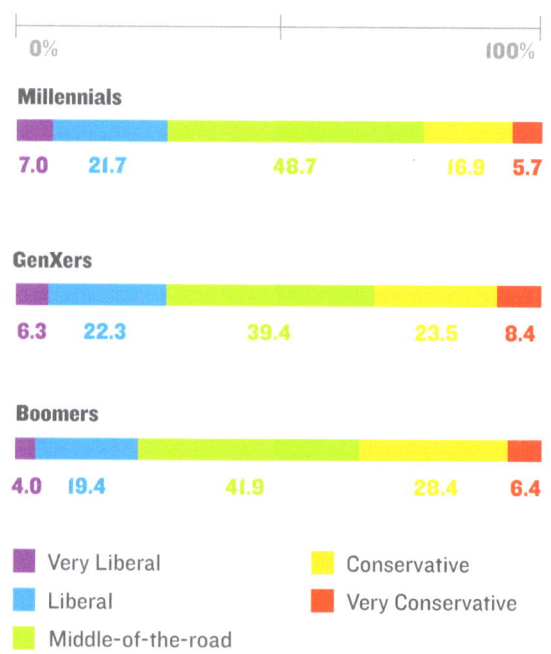

Figure 5b reports the generational findings for Latinos only. We see that U.S. Latinos (unlike African Americans) appear to be a potential voting bloc for Republicans, especially Latino GenXers, 45 percent of whom said they were likely to vote Republican.

We can sum up the political views and practices of Latinos in America as follows:

- **They, along with African Americans, were less likely to vote in the 2016 election than their white neighbors.**

- **Latinos are in fact the least politically engaged in this way, but we can say that they have the highest potential to increase their voter participation,** because they are the most likely to say that they aren't sure if they will vote or not. This indicates a potentially important voting bloc that both political parties may be able to motivate based on appropriate messaging and effective policy positions.

- **Older Americans are more likely than younger ones to vote, no matter their race/ethnicity.**

- **Latino respondents are more likely to identify as liberal than are African Americans or whites, though they are also more likely than African Americans to identify as conservative,** since over half of African Americans opt for middle-of-the-road. White respondents showed the greatest inclination toward voting Republican in 2016. Few African Americans expressed a preference for Republican candidates, but Latinos did indicate some level of interest, reinforcing the potential for Latinos to provide a substantial voting bloc for both major political parties.

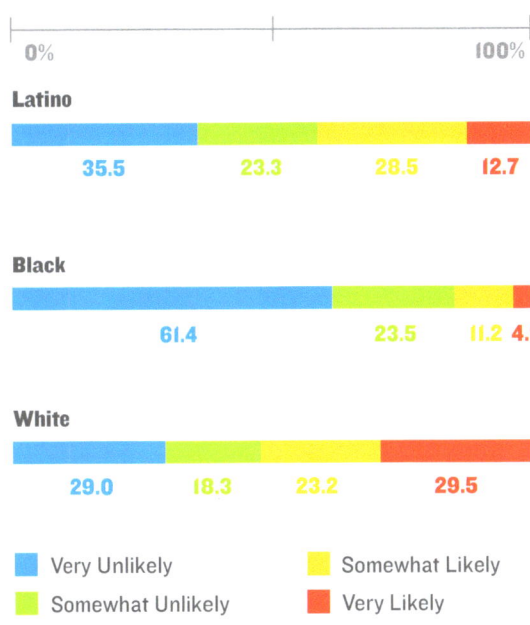

Figure 5a
Likelihood of Voting Republican in 2016, by Race/Ethnicity

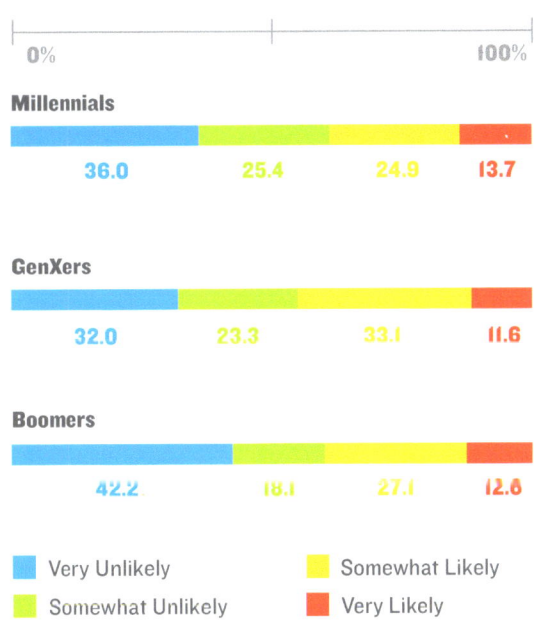

Figure 5b
Likelihood of Voting Republican in 2016 (Latino only)

LATINOS & THE CONSTITUTION

Opinions about the documents signed by early American leaders often reveal general ideas about the role, responsibility, and limits of the U.S. government. In an effort to delve deeper into public opinion, we asked respondents about their beliefs concerning the content of the U.S. Constitution and the Bill of Rights. Have these documents become "outdated," and hence in need of modification? Or do they continue to serve their proper functions and thus should be left alone? The question is, "do Americans still support the country's historical foundations, or not so much?"

Figure 6a suggests a solid majority of Americans—65 percent—believe that the founding documents should be left alone, without modification. This implies a basic level of acceptance and trust in the system of governance undergirding the American political system. A smaller share but still a significant minority—35 percent—who would favor amending founding documents may be less confident in the ability of these historical writings to speak to contemporary issues and concerns. It is important to break these numbers down and consider how race/ethnicity and age might affect views on this key issue.

Figure 6a

American Beliefs Regarding U.S. Founding Documents

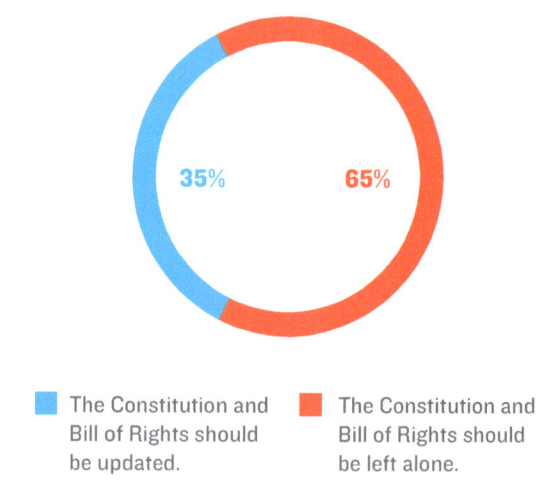

- The Constitution and Bill of Rights should be updated.
- The Constitution and Bill of Rights should be left alone.

How much do Americans still appreciate the key documents on which the republic stands?

Figure 6b displays results to this question by race/ethnicity. White Americans are the most likely to believe that the Constitution and the Bill of Rights should be left alone, while African Americans are most likely to take the opposite view. Just over half of all Latinos in America believe we should not revise these founding documents, but their opinions as a whole are much closer to those of African Americans than they are to whites. In short, the data suggest that white Americans are the group most confident in the enduring authority and relevance of the founding documents.

Lastly, Figure 6c displays results by generation for Latinos only. Beliefs are very similar across age groups—nearly 50/50 for everyone. This suggests that the responses of Latinos on this issue probably little affected the results from the general population (Figure 6a) one way or the other. Latinos are truly divided down the middle on this issue. Admittedly, it's an issue most of us probably don't think about much, and over which we have little or no power. We asked about it in order to get a sense of how much Americans still appreciate the key documents on which the republic stands.

Figure 6b
Beliefs about Founding Documents, by Race/Ethnicity

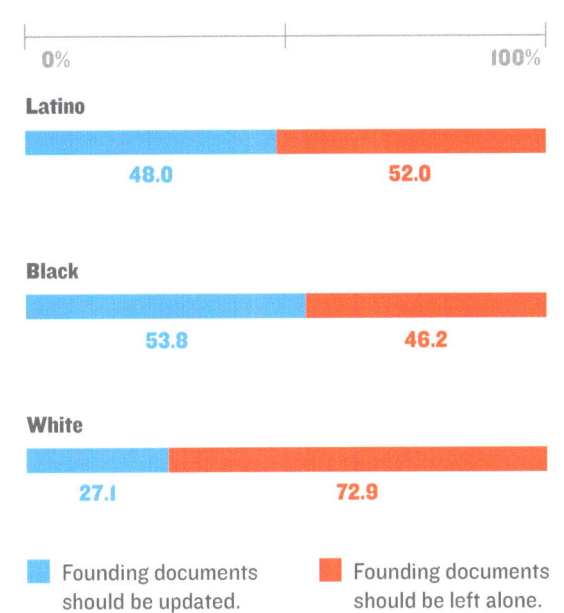

Figure 6c
Beliefs about Founding Documents, by Age Cohort (Latino only)

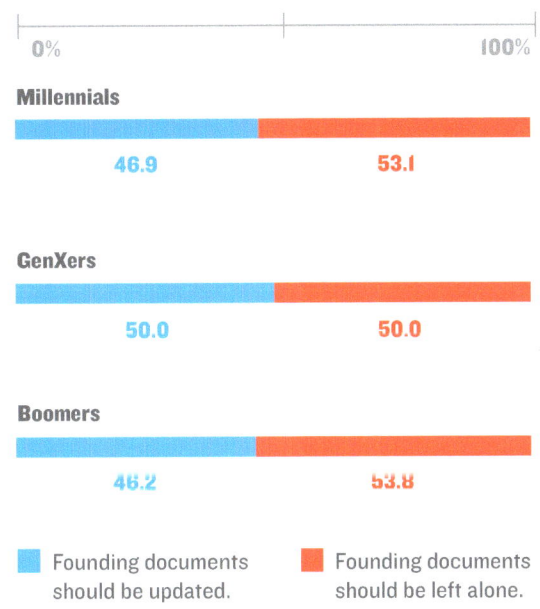

LATINOS & THE CONSTITUTION

FINDINGS FROM THE RELATIONSHIPS IN AMERICA SURVEY | 9

LATINO CIVIC KNOWLEDGE

Every year, well over half a million immigrants are naturalized and become permanent U.S. citizens. As part of that process, men and women study hard in order to exhibit an ample knowledge of American history and government. Our survey presented respondents with a four-question "pop quiz" about American history (in either English or Spanish, as preferred).

Take a look at the quiz, reproduced below. How would you score? However you did, you're not alone. Half of our respondents got at least two out of four questions right. But half of them couldn't. Overall, only 12 percent of Americans ages 18-60 answered all four questions correctly.

Figure 7 shows how Americans performed on the pop quiz, which we scored as 0 through 4. Figure 6a (p. 8) shows the overall percentages, while Figures 6b and 6c (p. 9) show a breakdown by the largest racial/ethnic groups making up our sample. Like with many pop quizzes in school, most people could answer at least half of the questions correctly.

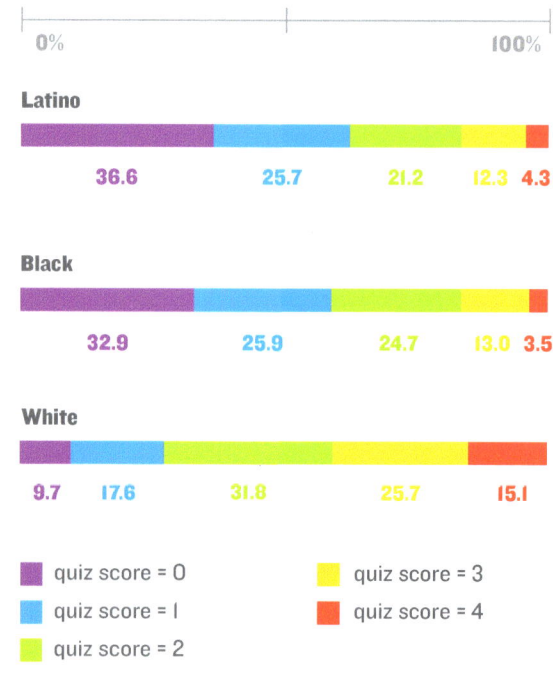

Figure 7

Combined Results of Survey Quiz on American History

FINDINGS FROM THE RELATIONSHIPS IN AMERICA SURVEY

Table 1
Survey Response Items Measuring Knowledge of American History

SURVEY QUIZ QUESTIONS ON AMERICAN HISTORY[9]

Now we'd like you to take a short, four-question "quiz" about American history. We'd much prefer if you would not stop to look for the answers, but rather simply move quickly through the questions relying only on your existing memory or knowledge of the answers. Remember, there is no penalty for answering incorrectly.

1. **The Declaration of Independence affirms that its citizens have "inalienable" and "natural" rights to all of the following except:**
   a. Property
   b. Liberty
   c. Pursuit of happiness
   d. Life
   e. I'm not sure.

2. **While there are many reasons why the colonists decided to rebel against British rule, the colonists declared independence in 1776 primarily in order to:**
   a. End the practice of slavery.
   b. Gain upward social mobility by ending Britain's aristocratic system.
   c. Have the right to freely exercise their religion.
   d. Stop having taxes and trade restrictions imposed without representation in Parliament.
   e. I'm not sure.

3. **Pick the answer that best describes why the nation's founders chose to establish a limited national government:**
   a. They believed the national government ought to have no power because "the government that governs best is the one that governs least."
   b. They believed that the states ought to be the primary governing bodies.
   c. They believed strongly that all men were created equal and so they abolished slavery.
   d. None of these are correct, since they did not establish a limited national government.
   e. I'm not sure.

4. **True or False: The Bill of Rights grants all rights to the states (or to the people) that are not explicitly granted to the federal government.**
   a. True
   b. False
   c. I'm not sure.

LATINO CIVIC KNOWLEDGE

Those who got three out of four right amounted to the same number—21 percent—as those who only answered one out of four questions correctly. Sadly, however, more people went scoreless—17 percent—than scored a perfect four out of four (12 percent).

Our results suggest a profound lack of awareness of the basics of American government history, but disproportionately so among minorities. About four white respondents received perfect scores for every one Latino or African American who did so. Members of minority groups often lack access to the types of educational experiences that might foster greater awareness of history and government, or may be more apt to witness contests over appropriate content for secondary history and government courses.

LATINO ECONOMIC VIEWS

The 1992 presidential election—when Bill Clinton defeated the Republican incumbent George H. W. Bush—is often remembered as one in which economic issues clearly trumped cultural and international concerns in the minds of many Americans. The now-famous slogan "The economy, stupid" has become a metaphor for the dominance of kitchen-table issues over high-minded theory (including foreign-policy disputes), things which no American politician has since been able to ignore. It also reminds us how inextricably linked is the political realm to the broader economy. In light of the recent elections—and the role that Latinos in America were poised to play in their outcomes—we do well to explore the political opinions and behaviors, as well as the views toward the U.S. economy, among this group.

Here we assess whether respondents generally held liberal or conservative economic views. Since most people have mixed feelings about economic issues, respondents were asked to report their opinions as a point on a continuum between two poles. Table 2 shows the exact wording of the questionnaire items, which were intended to capture whether individuals tended to agree more with free-market-oriented policies (conservative) or with the perspective that government regulation is best suited to manage the marketplace (progressive).[10]

Americans in general are most progressive on the question of extreme salary differentials.

Note that the conservative statements are on the "lower" end of the scale, and the progressive statements are on the "higher" end. We present results here by using average scores (between 1 and 7). In this case, a higher score represents greater overall acceptance of progressive or liberal economic values. A score right in the middle (leaning neither left nor right) would be a 4.

Figure 8 reports the average scores on these economic questions for whites, Blacks, and Latinos, as well as an "Overall" average score. At a glance, it suggests a moderate to slightly progressive outlook on issues related to government policy on the economy and the marketplace. There is no clear or strong association on the part of any race/ethnic group with either conservative or progressive economic values. White respondents, however, do hold the most conservative (and hence individualist) views of the three groups.

Latinos, like African Americans, are more inclined than whites to perceive free markets as unfair and more apt to be exploitative of the poor.[11] Similarly, Latinos and African Americans favor greater government regulation as a way to protect consumers, while whites prefer less government regulation over business.[12]

When the nation is approaching a presidential election, discussions regarding economic inequality and the concentration of wealth often take center stage as politicians vie for the sizable middle-class vote. For our study, we asked several questions directly related to issues of economic inequality. When compared to whites, Latinos and African Americans are more likely to agree with the idea that the gap between the highest wage earners and the lowest is too wide[13] and that government ought to have a "special claim" on "excessive profits."[14] White Americans, on the other hand, are more apt to feel that market forces rightly determine salary differences and that successful, high-wage earners already shoulder enough of the overall tax burden. Again, these are average scores across groups. As you can see, no group leans heavily in either direction on any question. Americans in general are most progressive on the question of extreme salary differentials.

Table 2
Survey Response Items Measuring Views of Government and Economy

Conservative Economic Values	1 2 3 4 5 6 7	Progressive Economic Values
Free markets reward individuals who create value for society.	○ ○ ○ ○ ○ ○ ○	Free markets allow the rich to exploit the poor.
People should be able to run their own businesses with as little governmental regulation as possible.	○ ○ ○ ○ ○ ○ ○	Government regulations serve a very important function in protecting consumers from bad business practices.
Salary differences in America can be explained logically based on supply and demand.	○ ○ ○ ○ ○ ○ ○	Salary differences in America are too extreme, with the top earners paid too much and the bottom too little.
People who are successful in business should not be required to pay more taxes than they currently do.	○ ○ ○ ○ ○ ○ ○	Governments should have a special claim on excessive profits earned by business owners.
Higher taxes should be avoided, even if that means we get fewer services.	○ ○ ○ ○ ○ ○ ○	Higher taxes are fine, so long as they are accompanied by more services.

LATINO ECONOMIC VIEWS

Even white Americans lean in the direction of suggesting that the top earners are paid too much and the bottom earners too little. Hence it is no surprise that inequality remains a live issue among a majority of Americans.

Finally, note the one area where white Americans, when compared to Latinos and African Americans, seem to hold the more liberal perspective on an economic issue. Whites are most likely to favor liberal taxation policies whereby paying higher taxes is acceptable on the condition that revenues from those taxes are used to provide public services.[15]

Figure 8
Average Scores on Government and Economy Questions, by Race/ethnicity

Conservative Economic Values		Progressive Economic Values
Free markets reward individuals who create value for society	All: 3.90 Latino: 4.30 Black: 4.28 White: 3.73	Free markets allow the rich to exploit the poor.
People should be able to run their own businesses with as little governmental regulation as possible.	All: 3.98 Latino: 4.43 Black: 4.47 White: 3.75	Government regulations serve a very important function in protecting consumers from bad business practices.
Salary differences in America can be explained logically based on supply and demand.	All: 4.66 Latino: 4.80 Black: 4.96 White: 4.56	Salary differences in America are too extreme, with the top earners paid too much and the bottom too little.
People who are successful in business should not be required to pay more taxes than they currently do.	All: 4.03 Latino: 4.32 Black: 4.41 White: 3.86	Governments should have a special claim on excessive profits earned by business owners.
Higher taxes should be avoided, even if that means we get fewer services.	All: 4.06 Latino: 3.89 Black: 3.92 White: 4.15	Higher taxes are fine, so long as they are accompanied by more services.

■ All   ■ Latino   ■ Black   ■ White

LATINOS & RELIGION

While faith traditions other than some type of Christianity remain in the minority in America, a growing number of people do not report any specific religious affiliation at all. Among the present study sample of 15,738 individuals who provided information on religious affiliation, 34 percent were Protestant, 22 percent are Catholic, 13 percent are unaffiliated, and 31 percent fall into another category or are undecided.

When we look at religious affiliation by racial/ethnic background (shown in Figure 9), several findings stand out. As expected, the majority of Latinos were Catholic, while whites and African Americans were primarily concentrated in Protestant denominations. Note the relatively high percentage of white Americans who report no religious affiliation at all, more than double the percent of Latinos and more than triple that of African Americans. Agnosticism and atheism were far more characteristic of white (survey) respondents than of others.

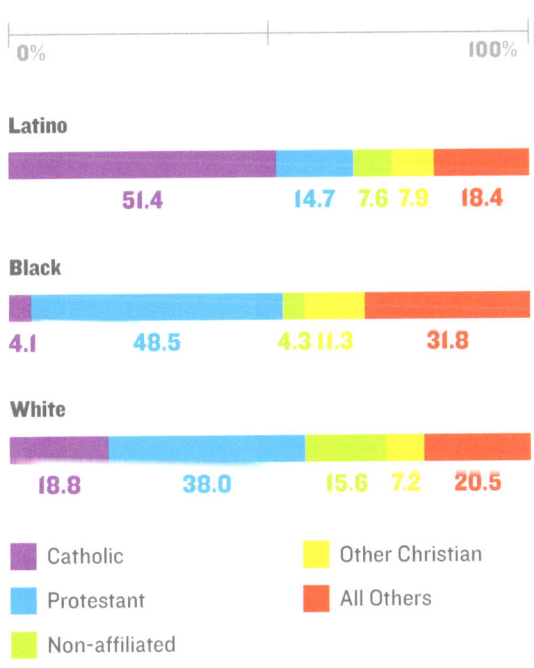

Figure 9
Religious Affiliation, by Race/Ethnicity

Latino: 51.4 | 14.7 | 7.6 | 7.9 | 18.4
Black: 4.1 | 48.5 | 4.3 | 11.3 | 31.8
White: 18.8 | 38.0 | 15.6 | 7.2 | 20.5

- Catholic
- Protestant
- Non-affiliated
- Other Christian
- All Others

Christianity, however, is a rather large umbrella faith, and those who gather under it hold many different perspectives. Mainline Protestants make up a large proportion of Americans and may include members of large Christian denominations like Presbyterians, American Baptists, and Lutherans. Compared to other Christian churches, these traditions are characterized by less "literalist" understandings of scripture, and they may offer comparatively greater levels of accommodation to the prevailing cultural norms. They often attract a more highly educated, wealthier, and more suburban constituency.

We're becoming a bipolar nation when it comes to religiosity.

Evangelicals typically embrace more "literalist" and absolute beliefs than do mainline Protestants regarding doctrine as well as regarding social issues like cohabitation, same-sex marriage, and abortion. Fundamentalists would plot themselves even farther away from Mainliners, although their civic involvement is typically less active than that of Evangelicals, whose views often translate into political engagement.[16]

Liberal Protestants include members of denominations, including Episcopalian and the United Church of Christ, that typically apply more fluid interpretations of biblical doctrine.[17] These churches tend to make fewer demands on congregants in terms of lifestyle choices, expected attendance, and participation, and place less emphasis on moral mandates.

Finally, Pentecostalism is a growing and global movement that emphasizes baptism, public acceptance of Christ, and spiritual experiences as key signals of salvation. Pentecostals often characterize their daily lives as revolving around religious expectations and commitments, and are willing to accept social stigma for accepting views that may run quite counter to the dominant culture.[18]

Figure 10
Theological Identification, by Race/Ethnicity

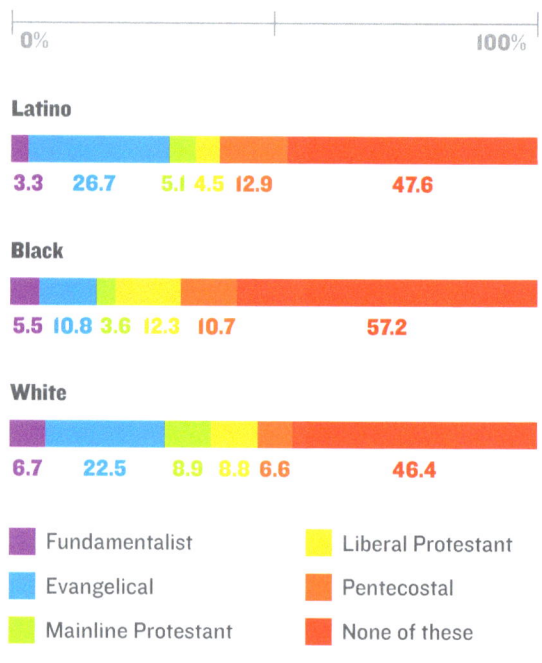

Figure 10 shows the distribution of these Protestant theological orientations by race/ethnicity in America, keeping in mind that we're not talking about the half of all Latinos that identify as Roman Catholic. The highest share of self-proclaimed evangelicals is actually found among Latinos, not whites (who trail them slightly). Taking into account what we know about the political orientation of the Evangelical movement—and keeping in mind the findings above, which reveal the potential for increased political engagement among Latinos—it stands to reason that Latino evangelicals may represent a constituency that is both socially conservative and poised to be motivated into greater political participation.

Corresponding to the appeal of Pentecostalism in Latin American countries,[19] our sample shows that the highest percentage of U.S. Pentecostals are Latino (13 percent), followed by African Americans (11 percent) and then whites (7 percent).

Of course, even within a denomination or affiliation, personal practices and views (both theologically and politically) can vary widely. We asked questions on a series of religious issues, starting with a common one about overall religiosity. Patterns are shown in the chart below (Figure 11) and lend support to the general consensus that Americans indeed remain rather religious when contrasted to other Western nations.

Almost half of all Americans say religion is very important in their lives.

Figure 11
"How important (if at all) is religious faith to you?"

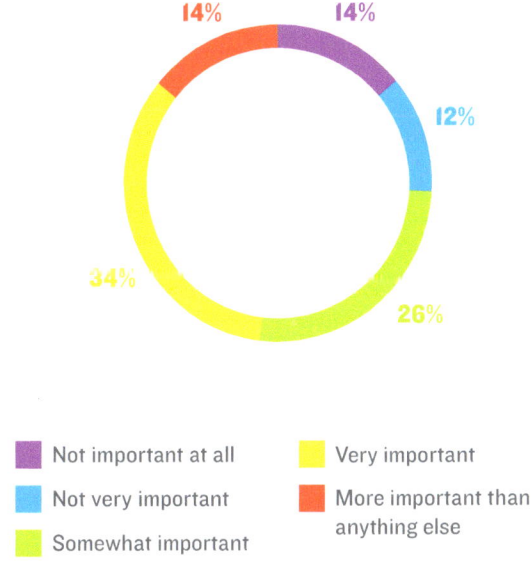

- Not important at all: 14%
- Not very important: 12%
- Somewhat important: 26%
- Very important: 34%
- More important than anything else: 14%

While one in seven (14 percent) Americans told us that religion is more important than anything else in their lives, when we combine that with those who say religion is "very important," the total percentage jumps to almost half (48 percent) of all Americans. In contrast, far more modest percentages feel that religion is either "not very" or "not important at all." When we look at race/ethnicity, Table 3 shows that African Americans stand out as having the highest levels of personal piety, and when we combine the "very important" and the "more important than anything else" measure, a clear majority of African Americans attest to religion's key significance in their lives, followed by Latinos and (less than half of) whites.

Table 3
Survey Response Items Measuring the Importance of Religious Faith, by Race/Ethnicity

"How important (if at all) is religious faith to you?"	White	Black	Latino
Not important at all	17%	6%	9%
Not very important	13%	5%	8%
Somewhat important	25%	19%	29%
Very important	31%	48%	40%
More important than anything else	13%	21%	15%
Combined both "very important" and "more important than anything else"	44%	69%	55%

Figure 12
Regular Attendance at Religious Services

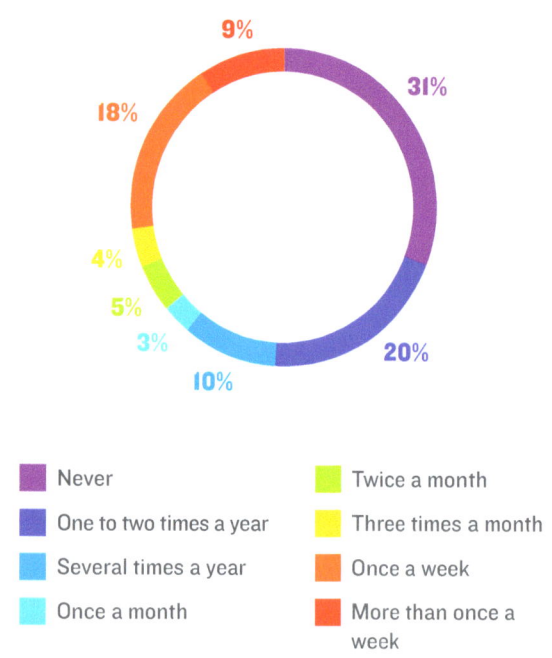

- Never
- One to two times a year
- Several times a year
- Once a month
- Twice a month
- Three times a month
- Once a week
- More than once a week

Research has indicated (and common sense affirms) that active churchgoers tend to hold firmer religious beliefs and are more likely to follow religious precepts than those who attend religious services less regularly. With this in mind, we prompted respondents with the following question: "How often, if ever, do you normally attend religious services (not counting weddings, baptisms, and funerals)?"

As shown by Figure 12, most Americans still do attend religious services, even if that attendance is best described as infrequent or sporadic. Interestingly, approximately 60 percent are concentrated—roughly equally—at the outermost categories, suggesting that large percentages of Americans attend religious services either regularly (once a week or more) or not at all. Indeed, we're becoming a bipolar nation when it comes to religiosity. Another 30 percent report occasional attendance throughout the year (one to several times per year), which may suggest religious attendance that is predicated on the occurrence of religious holidays and other special events.

How does religiosity vary by race/ethnicity? As shown by Figure 13, there is a sizable proportion of white Americans who never attend religious services, representing a significantly higher percentage than either African Americans or Latinos. African Americans, meanwhile, are more likely than others to attend church more than once per week, followed closely by Latinos.

Figure 13
Religious Attendance, by Race/Ethnicity

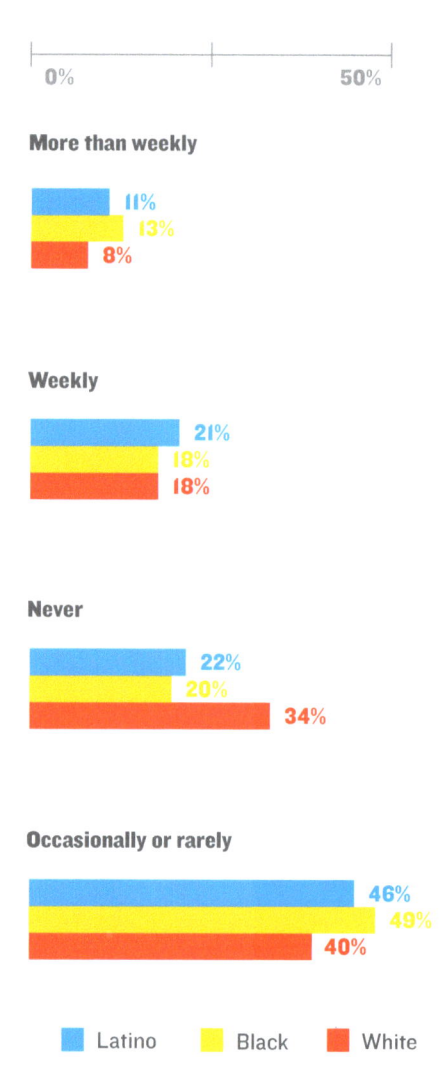

FINDINGS FROM THE RELATIONSHIPS IN AMERICA SURVEY

These results provide insight into the way that race and ethnicity shape religious piety among Americans. The results of the survey data provide evidence for the following conclusions:

1. Most Americans either attend church regularly or not at all. We are a nation exhibiting a religious "split personality."

2. African Americans are, overall, more actively religious than either Latinos or whites.

3. Nevertheless, roughly equal percentages of white, African American, and Latino Americans attend church weekly.

Specific theological beliefs held by individuals—as well as changes in personal religiosity over time—can also be measured through pointed questions. Respondents were asked the following questions:

- "Compared to ten years ago, are you more or less active in organized religion today?"

- "Do you think there is a real heaven and a real hell?"

- "Do you think there is life, or some sort of conscious existence, after death? If you're unsure, pick the answer that's closest to your best guess."

- "Do you think there will be a bodily resurrection, that is, where the bodies of deceased persons will rise again?"

Most Americans attend church regularly or not at all. We are a nation exhibiting a religious "split personality."

LATINOS & RELIGION

These data reinforce what social scientists have been writing about for decades: in the United States, religion matters.

Figure 14 offers an overview of responses to these questions categorized into the major racial/ethnic groups making up our study sample.

The majority of Americans, regardless of race/ethnicity, (still) believe in the existence of both heaven and hell. However, the largest percentage of these believers is found among African Americans, at 84 percent—a substantially higher proportion than for whites (68 percent) or Latinos (70 percent). All groups show a strong general belief in life after death. African Americans and Latinos are also more likely to report increased religiosity over the past ten years, while most whites report an unchanged level of involvement. When it comes to a bodily resurrection, African Americans hold significantly stronger beliefs when compared to both whites and Latinos.

All told, these data reinforce what social scientists have been writing about for decades: in the United States, religion matters. Americans are characterized by high levels of belief in supernatural phenomena and highly theological principles such as the resurrection of the body. African Americans, as multiple studies have shown, represent the most religious group of Americans, followed by Latinos. Most whites are also religious, but less active in a church.

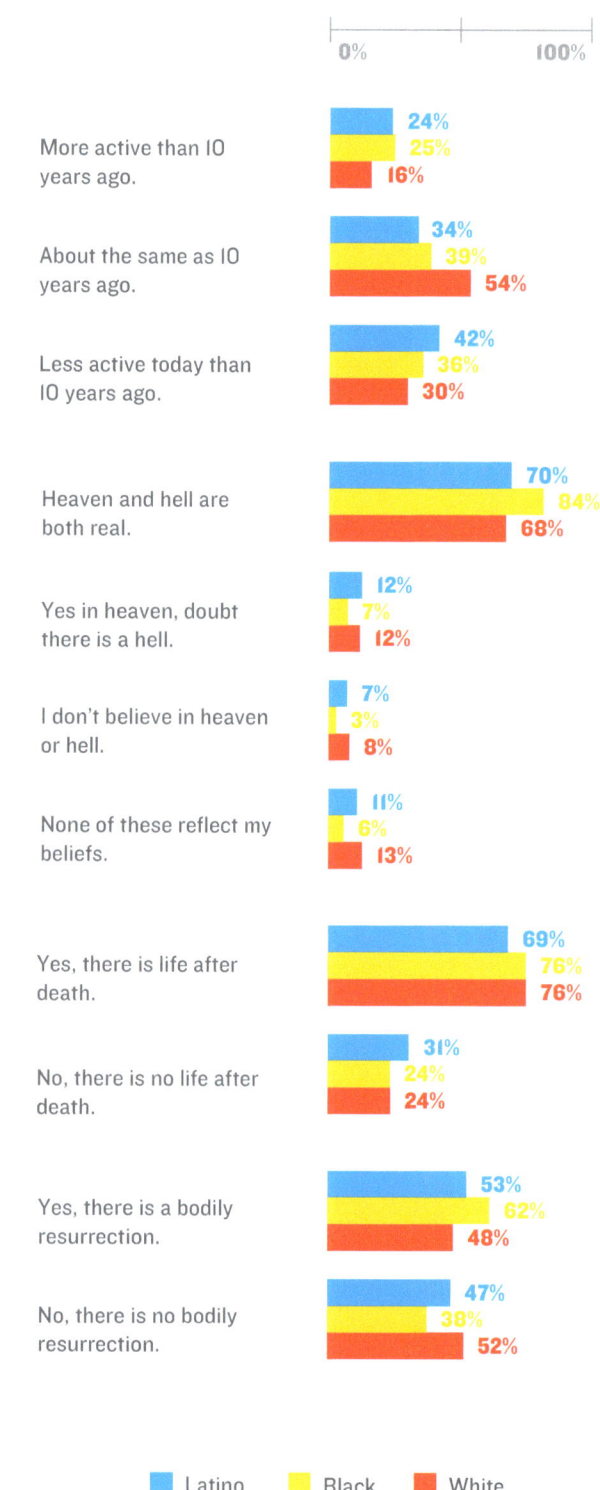

Figure 14
Changing Religiosity and Theological Beliefs, by Race/Ethnicity

	Latino	Black	White
More active than 10 years ago.	24%	25%	16%
About the same as 10 years ago.	34%	39%	54%
Less active today than 10 years ago.	42%	36%	30%
Heaven and hell are both real.	70%	84%	68%
Yes in heaven, doubt there is a hell.	12%	7%	12%
I don't believe in heaven or hell.	7%	3%	8%
None of these reflect my beliefs.	11%	6%	13%
Yes, there is life after death.	69%	76%	76%
No, there is no life after death.	31%	24%	24%
Yes, there is a bodily resurrection.	53%	62%	48%
No, there is no bodily resurrection.	47%	38%	52%

LATINO FAMILIES

Social scientists who focus on the millions of Latinos in America continue to find that the institution of family is central to their everyday experiences.[20] In fact, the term "Latino familialism" has been used to denote the pivotal role that family plays in the lives of many Latino households.[21] RIA asked respondents about both their childhood family experiences and their views of the family as a social institution. The answers we heard from Latinos seem to support that familist stereotype.

Figure 15 shows the respondents' level of agreement with three statements related to positive family interactions during childhood.

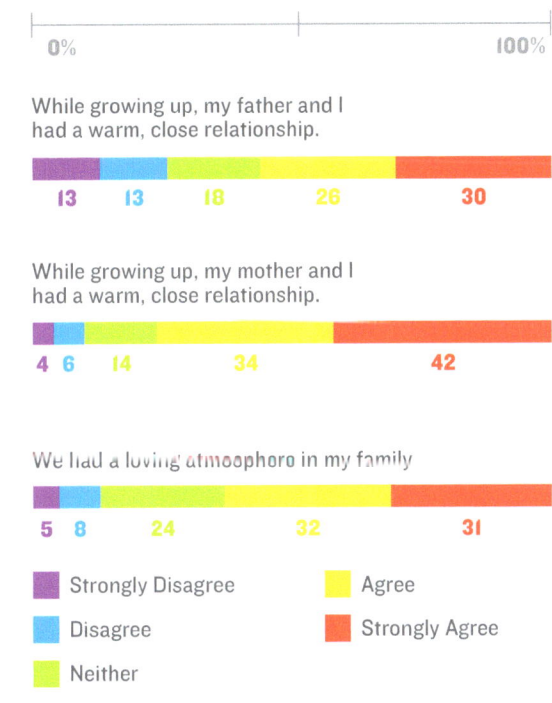

Figure 15
Positive Childhood Family Experiences among Latinos

While growing up, my father and I had a warm, close relationship.

| 13 | 13 | 18 | 26 | 30 |

While growing up, my mother and I had a warm, close relationship.

| 4 | 6 | 14 | 34 | 42 |

We had a loving atmosphere in my family

| 5 | 8 | 24 | 32 | 31 |

- Strongly Disagree
- Disagree
- Neither
- Agree
- Strongly Agree

We also asked respondents about the negative effects of childhood experiences and how these experiences might have carried over into adulthood. In light of the high percentages reporting positive childhood family life, our results for Latinos on this question are not surprising:

- A minority of Latinos report unstable family relationships in childhood or negative effects in their adult lives from their upbringing.

Figure 16

Latinos' Parent-Child Relationships, by Sex

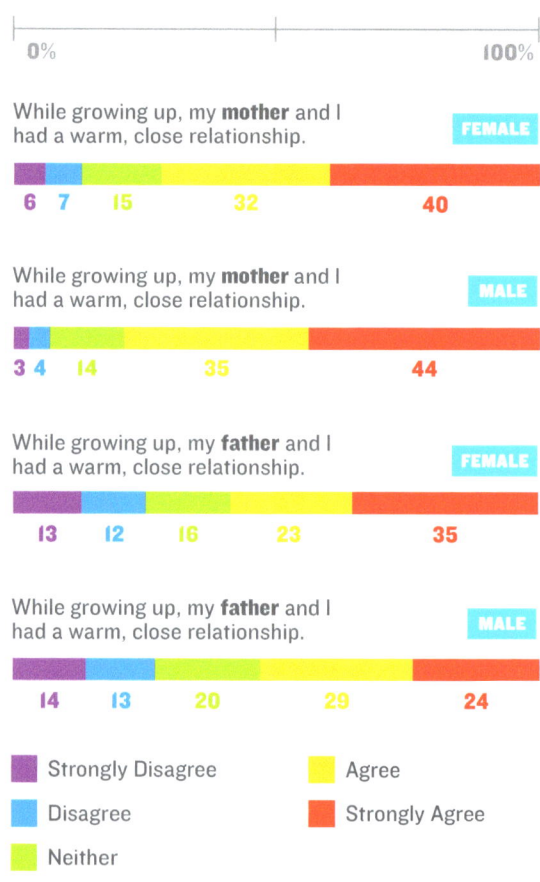

A slight majority of respondents "strongly agree"" or "agree" that they had a warm, close relationship with their father, while over 75 percent feel this way about their mother. Similarly, over 60 percent of them would say that they grew up in a loving family atmosphere. We wondered, however, who is warm and close with whom? Does the sex of the child and the parent matter?

As shown in Figure 16, the son and daughter responses related to mothers are strikingly similar. The percentage of females who either "strongly agreed" or "agreed" that they shared a warm, close relationship with their mother was 72 percent, and Latinos (males) responded at a slightly higher 79 percent. Our statistical tests indicate that this difference is not sizable enough to warrant the suggestion that there is any difference between Latino men and women when it comes to positive childhood relationships with their mothers.

The percentage of Latinas who either "strongly agreed" or "agreed" that they shared a warm, close relationship with their fathers is 58 percent; for Latinos, it is somewhat lower at 53 percent. However, a significantly higher percent of Latinas (35%) "strongly agree" with this statement when compared to men (24%).

- While equal numbers of Latino men and women report warm and close relationships with their mothers, Latina women tend to show a higher level of closeness to their fathers than do Latino men.[22][23]

Figure 17 again shows three questions asked of Latinos, along with the five possible measures that could be chosen. The first two questions are about negative experiences in childhood and implications for their adult lives. The third question seeks to measure instability in childhood life, a key factor in negative outcomes for children (such as drug use and depression). Note that for all three questions, only a minority of Latinos reported negative experiences or feelings.

The most popular indicator of difficult family history is the first of these: 31 percent of Latinos "strongly agree" or "agree" that "there are matters from my family experience that I'm still having trouble dealing with or coming to terms with." Twenty-two (22) percent agreed that "there are matters from my family experience that negatively affect my ability to form close relationships." Finally, 16 percent labeled their family relationships as "confusing, inconsistent, and unpredictable."

Generally Latinos have positive childhood experiences characterized by solid ties with parents.

Overall, the general trend in the data indicates that Latinos have experienced positive childhood experiences characterized by solid ties with parents, stable family dynamics, and minimal psychological or emotional stress that carries into adulthood.

Another series of questions we asked have less to do with childhood family experiences and more with overall attitudes toward the family as a social institution. We particularly wanted to understand whether Latinos tend to hold more traditional or more progressive views of the family and what factors might shape the ways that Latinos think about the place of the family in contemporary society.

Figure 17

Negative Childhood Family Experiences among Latinos

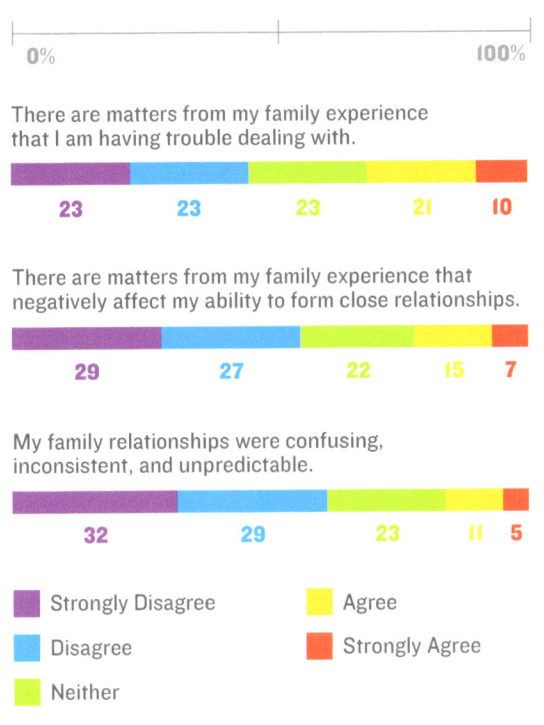

FINDINGS FROM THE RELATIONSHIPS IN AMERICA SURVEY

LATINO MARRIAGE & FAMILIES

There is much discussion in both academic research and the popular media about the traditional family and conventional "family values." Many have argued that nuclear families—made up of two married, heterosexual adults open to children—are the most historically enduring and the optimal environment in which to raise future citizens. Furthermore, traditional families are understood as central to the stability of society as a whole—its basic building block.

Proponents of changing family norms, on the other hand, argue that the idea of family is open to interpretation, particularly in light of increased divorce rates, greater acceptance of same-sex relationships, and a growing liberation of women. Such a perspective would emphasize the individuality of families and argue that successful families are based on nurturing and love (and in some cases, the value of independence), not on particular roles or structures. Recent relationship trends suggest that more and more Americans approve of—and are choosing—nontraditional forms of romantic attachment.[24] These may include cohabiting in lieu of marriage, same-sex marriage and family formation, and for a small but growing number, polyamorous relationships among multiple partners.

> **Traditional families are understood as central to the stability of society as a whole—its basic building block.**

For many Americans, the idea of "marriage" is simply no longer salient. At the most extreme, marriage is seen as the enemy of happiness. One writer posits polyamory (where "no one is responsible for anyone else's emotions or meeting anyone else's needs") as a "desirable alternative to the wedded misery" she sees all around her.[25]

We explored public opinion on this topic via a series of questions in which we asked respondents to tell us what they thought of seven statements about marriage and relationships:

1. **Marriage is an outdated institution.**

2. **It is a good idea for couples considering marriage to live together in order to decide whether or not they get along well enough to be married to one another.**

3. **It is OK for two people to get together for sex and not necessarily expect anything further.**

4. **It should be legal for gays and lesbians to marry in America.**

5. **If a couple has children, they should stay married unless there is physical or emotional abuse.**

6. **It is sometimes permissible for a married person to have sex with someone other than his/her spouse.**[26]

7. **It is OK for three or more consenting adults to live together in a sexual/romantic relationship.**

Higher scores (on a scale of 1 to 5) indicate more traditional views of family life overall.

We calculated the average score for all seven items to create an Index of Marriage and Family Attitudes (IMFA). As shown by Figure 18, the scores on the IMFA indicate that Latinos hold more traditional views than do their white and African American counterparts. Furthermore, Latinos are the only group to have scored higher (and hence more traditional) than the overall average. And while these differences may seem modest, tests indicate that they are statistically significant.[27]

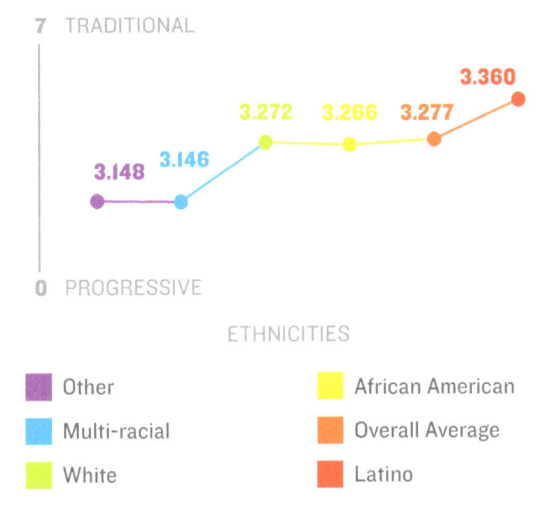

Figure 18

Average Scores on Index of Marriage and Family Attitudes, by Race/Ethnicity

7 TRADITIONAL

Other: 3.148
Multi-racial: 3.146
White: 3.272
African American: 3.266
Overall Average: 3.277
Latino: 3.360

0 PROGRESSIVE

ETHNICITIES

- Other
- Multi-racial
- White
- African American
- Overall Average
- Latino

LATINO MARRIAGE & FAMILIES

Latinos hold differing views about marriage and family, based on national origin.

Keeping in mind the higher levels of family traditionalism among Latinos, we next wanted to assess additional factors that might shape these views. Fortunately, the substantial size of our study sample allowed us to separate Latinos by the source of their national origin. As shown by Figure 19, in keeping with general demographic trends in American society as a whole, the largest percentage of Latinos in our sample reported either U.S. or Mexican origin.

Figure 20 shows average IMFA index scores for Latinos, by country of origin. Here we see results that run counter to expectations of Latinos as a monolithic demographic bloc; they hold differing views about marriage and family, based on national origin. U.S.-born and South American Latinos hold more progressive attitudes than those of Mexican and Central American origin. (Again, more complex statistical tests indicate this to be a significant difference.[28]) We might deduce that the popular culture and the religious context of Latinos' countries of origin may very well shape their outlook. (These data are unable to speak directly to this theory.) This result led us to consider other factors (such as age of respondent) that might shape the views of Latinos when it comes to marriage and family dynamics.

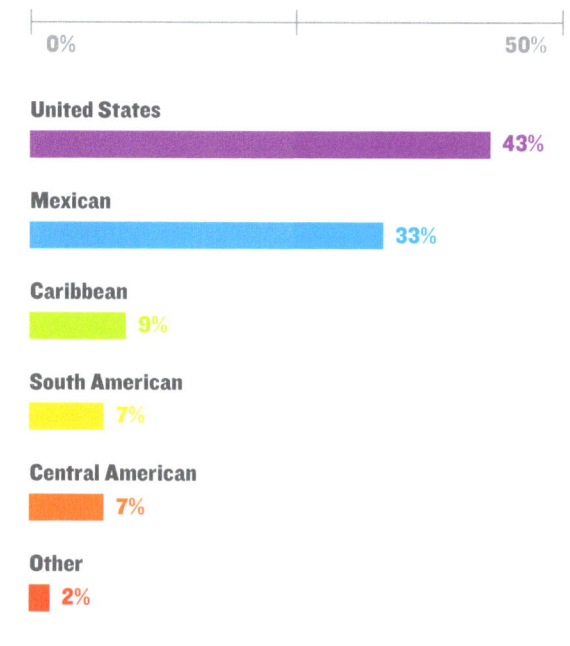

Figure 19

Latinos' Country of Origin, by Percentage

- United States: 43%
- Mexican: 33%
- Caribbean: 9%
- South American: 7%
- Central American: 7%
- Other: 2%

Latino Nationality (N=2,591)

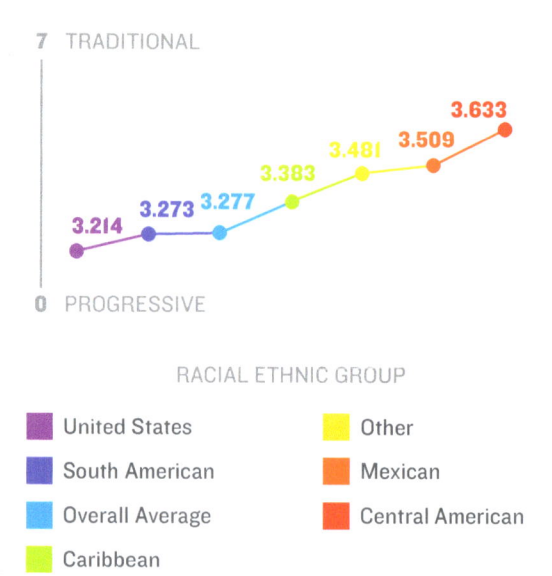

Figure 20

Average Scores on Views toward Marriage and Family, by Latino Nationality

- United States: 3.214
- South American: 3.273
- Overall Average: 3.277
- Caribbean: 3.383
- Other: 3.481
- Mexican: 3.509
- Central American: 3.633

RACIAL ETHNIC GROUP

Most Americans think the institution of marriage has a future.

It has been suggested by social scientists and pollsters that younger Americans tend to hold more progressive social values on a host of issues like same-sex marriage, marital relationships, and sexual norms.[29] We put this proposition to the test using IMFA scores to assess the effects of age on views toward marriage and family issues among Latino Americans. Figure 21 shows a clear pattern whereby age is indeed associated with variation in attitudes. Particularly noteworthy is the fact that younger Latino Millennials (under thirty years of age) show markedly less traditional attitudes than those of their older counterparts.[30]

Is Marriage Relevant?

In addition to creating the index, we compared responses to certain specific questions on the topic of modern family structures, by three key characteristics: race/ethnicity, birth cohort, and the preferred language in the home. Figures 22a and 22b report respondents' levels of agreement that "marriage is an outdated institution." They reveal that regardless of race, Americans largely disagree that the institution of marriage is an irrelevant, "outdated" social institution. That is, most Americans think the institution of marriage has a future.

However, the percentage of whites who "strongly disagree" or "disagree" with the idea that marriage is outdated (72 percent) is much higher than that of African Americans (56 percent) and Latinos (52 percent). Also, African Americans and Latinos have nearly identical percentages of neutral responses, neither agreeing nor disagreeing with this statement. Whites are more decided on the matter (Figure 22a).

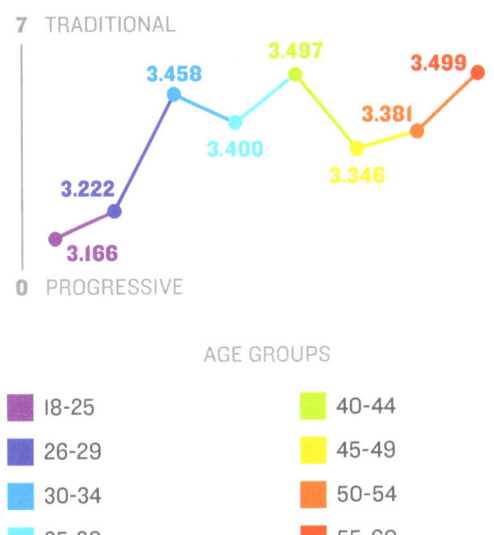

Figure 21
Average Scores on Views toward Marriage and Family among Latinos, by Age

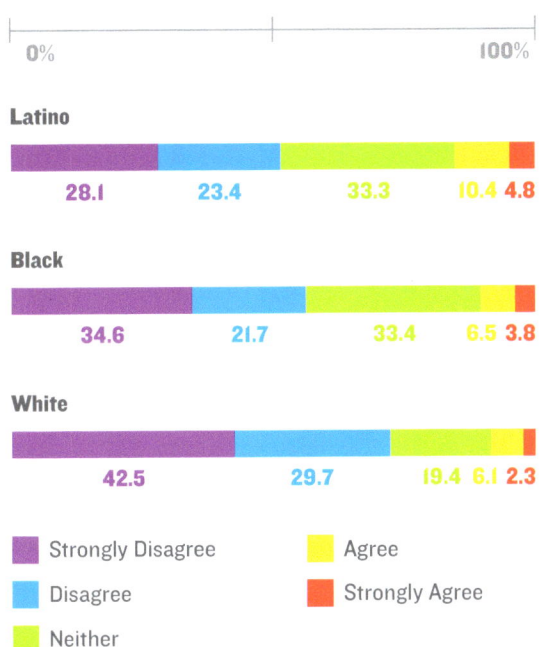

Figure 22a
"Marriage is an Outdated Institution," by Race/Ethnicity

Older respondents were predictably more likely to believe that marriage is not outdated. When we looked specifically at Latinos by generation (Figure 22b), the same pattern held but with greater differences between the Boomers and the younger generations. Just under two-thirds of Latino Boomers (64 percent) disagreed, while just under half (49 percent) of GenXers and Millennials said the same.

Age plays an important role in shaping attitudes toward marriage in America—and this is especially true among Latinos. Latino Millennials and GenXers are considerably less traditional (and looking at the "neither" measure, less decided) than are their older relatives about the significance of marriage in modern life.

Spanish-speaking households generally hold more traditional views on issues related to the family.

We might expect households where Spanish is the primary language to hold more traditional values on this and other family related issues. Figure 22c indicates a moderate effect related to primary household language, but the relationship is somewhat counter-intuitive. Individuals in predominantly Spanish-speaking households have somewhat greater agreement and are less likely to have a firm opinion on the idea that marriage is an outdated institution. However, on most other family and marriage issues, respondents from predominantly Spanish-speaking households generally hold more traditional views on issues related to the family.

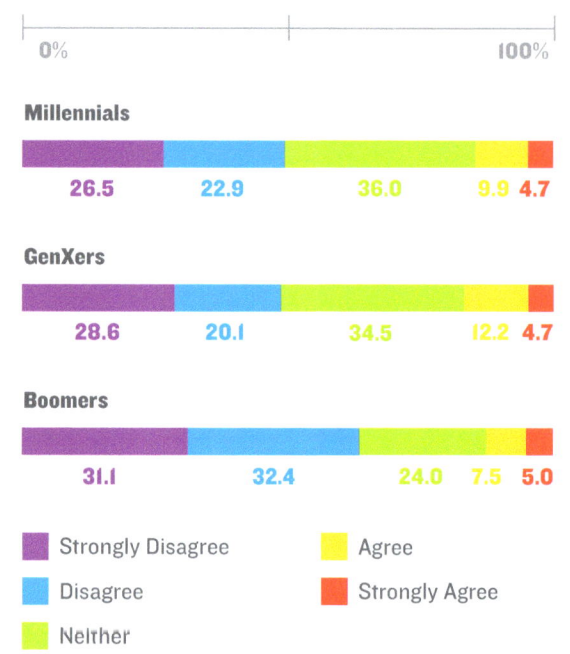

Figure 22b

Marriage Is an Outdated Institution, by Birth Cohort (Latinos only)

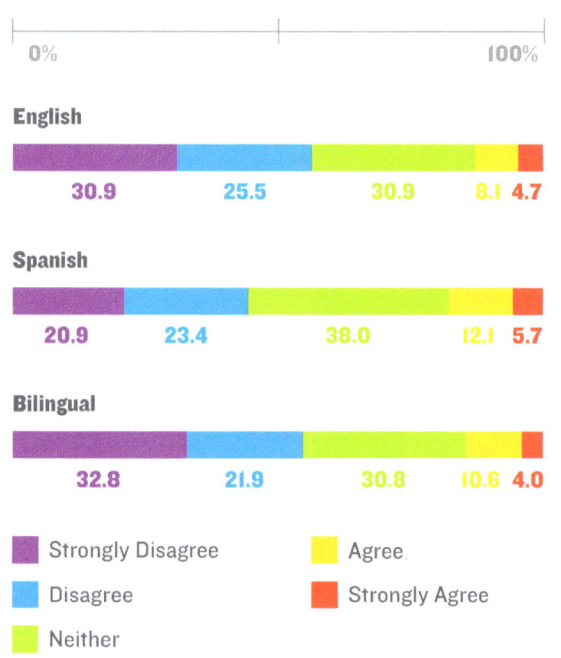

Figure 22c

Marriage Is an Outdated Institution, by Primary Household Language (Latinos only)

FINDINGS FROM THE RELATIONSHIPS IN AMERICA SURVEY

What about Cohabitation?

Research continues to reveal that more Americans are living together before marriage.[31] Our study asked to what extent respondents agreed or disagreed with this statement: "It is a good idea for couples considering marriage to live together in order to decide whether or not they get along well enough to be married to one another."

Levels of agreement, disagreement, and indifference were similar across racial/ethnic groups (Figure 23a), though African Americans were the least likely to support cohabitation. At the same time, they were also the most undecided ("neither") on the matter. Latinos fell between the other two groups on both counts.

When looking only at Latinos (Figure 23b), we found minimal differences based on when one was born. Latino Millennials appear to be slightly more supportive overall of cohabitation when compared to GenXers and Baby Boomers. It is possible that Latino Millennials are more supportive of cohabitation before marriage as an economically beneficial option available to them during times of financial duress. Latinos as a whole were most adversely impacted by the financial downturn of 2008, and Millennials are more likely than other generations to be unmarried.[32] In contrast, GenXers grew up in a time when the United States was experiencing high levels of economic prosperity. As more Latino Millennials transition into adulthood, we may see an increase in their support for cohabitation before marriage.

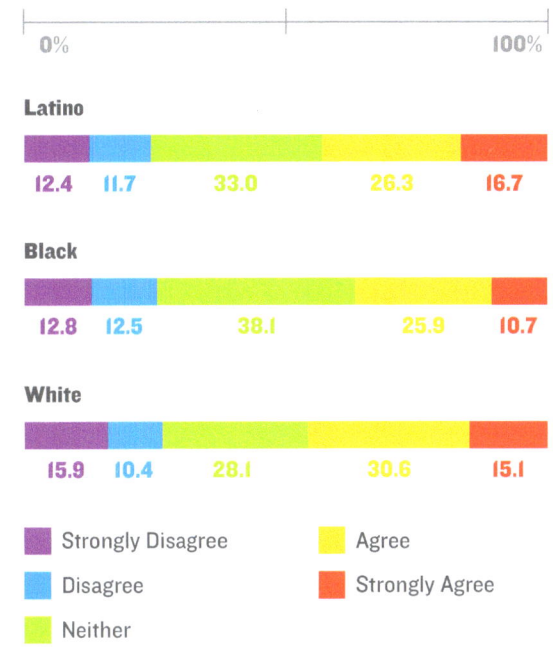

Figure 23a

Level of Support for Cohabitation before Marriage, by Race/Ethnicity

Latino: 12.4 | 11.7 | 33.0 | 26.3 | 16.7
Black: 12.8 | 12.5 | 38.1 | 25.9 | 10.7
White: 15.9 | 10.4 | 28.1 | 30.6 | 15.1

- Strongly Disagree
- Disagree
- Neither
- Agree
- Strongly Agree

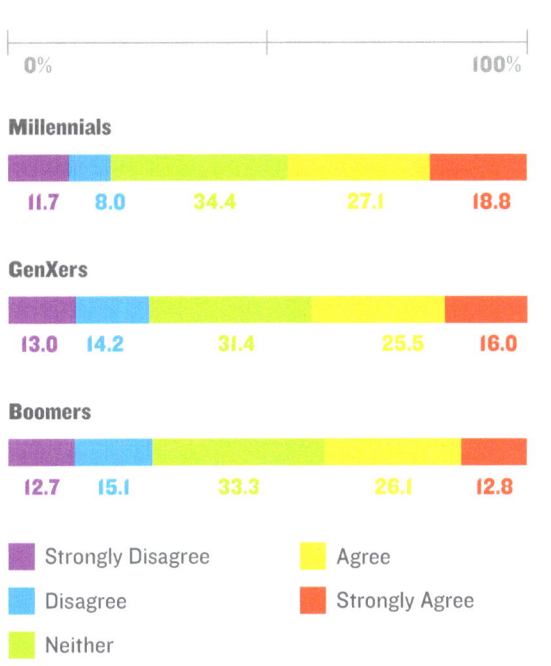

Figure 23b

Level of Agreement for Cohabitation before Marriage, by Birth Cohort (Latinos only)

Millennials: 11.7 | 8.0 | 34.4 | 27.1 | 18.8
GenXers: 13.0 | 14.2 | 31.4 | 25.5 | 16.0
Boomers: 12.7 | 15.1 | 33.3 | 26.1 | 12.8

- Strongly Disagree
- Disagree
- Neither
- Agree
- Strongly Agree

LATINO MARRIAGE & FAMILIES

Spanish-dominant households are the most likely to disagree with cohabitation before marriage.

In terms of cohabitation and primary language spoken in the household, individuals who reside in homes where Spanish is the primary language hold more traditional views on this question. As Figure 23c demonstrates, Spanish-dominant households are the most likely to disagree with cohabitation before marriage.

Figure 23c

Level of Agreement for Cohabitation before Marriage, by Primary Household (Latinos only)

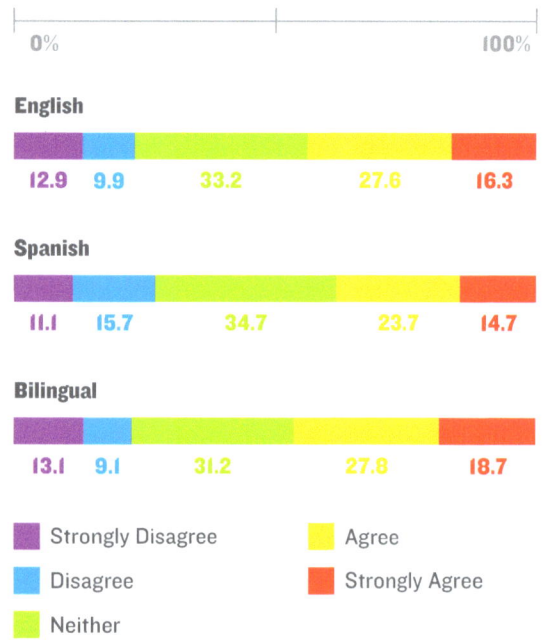

Does Sex Require Commitment?

Postponing sex until marriage is a core principle of traditional marital values.[33] However, some have challenged this notion by arguing that premarital sex and cohabitation are now part of the conventional courtship process toward marriage in most industrial societies.[34] We asked respondents to signal their agreement or disagreement with this statement: "It is OK for two people to get together for sex and not necessarily expect anything further."

Figure 24a reveals that a higher percentage of whites agree that "no strings attached" sex is acceptable, when compared to African Americans and Latinos. Like with cohabitation, a higher percentage of African Americans report indifference or indecision on this issue.

Figure 24a

Level of Support for Casual/Uncommitted Sex, by Race/Ethnicity

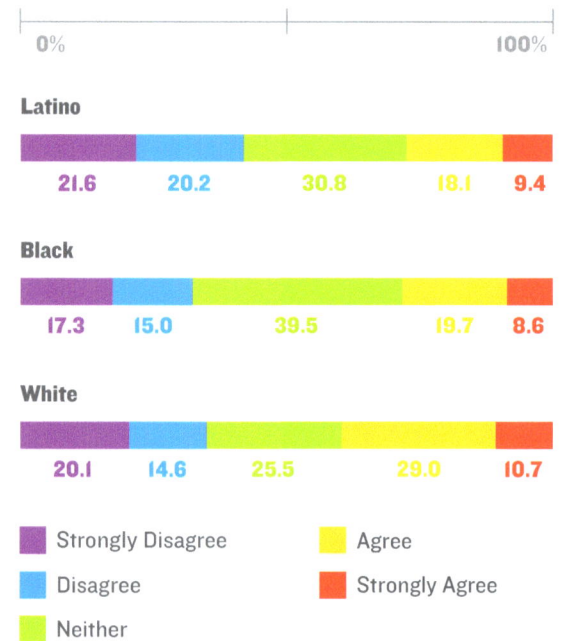

Curiously, answers to the question were pretty evenly distributed across the generations (results not shown). Millennials, however, were more likely than others to strongly support it.

Figure 24b, which specifically divides Latinos by generation, reveals that Latinos are less supportive of casual sex than is the population as a whole. Thirty-one (31) percent of Latino Millennials agree that casual sex is okay (compared to 37 percent of Millennials in general). The same is true of only 23 percent of Latino GenXers and 28 percent of Latino Boomers. Each is lower than its counterparts in the overall population, indicating that support for "no strings attached" sex is lower among Latinos than non-Latinos.

The results are more striking when we look at Spanish-dominant households. The majority of Spanish-speaking households disapprove of casual sex, with over half of respondents saying they strongly disagree or disagree that casual sex is acceptable. Meanwhile, English and bilingual households are similar in terms of support for casual sex (Figure 24c).

The majority of Spanish-speaking households disapprove of casual sex.

Figure 24b
Level of Support for Casual/Uncommitted Sex, by Birth Cohort (Latino only)

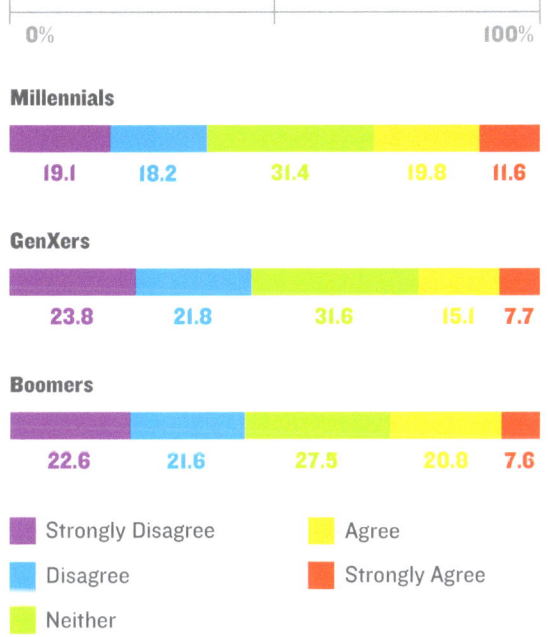

Figure 24c
Level of Support for Casual/Uncommitted Sex, by Primary Household Language (Latino only)

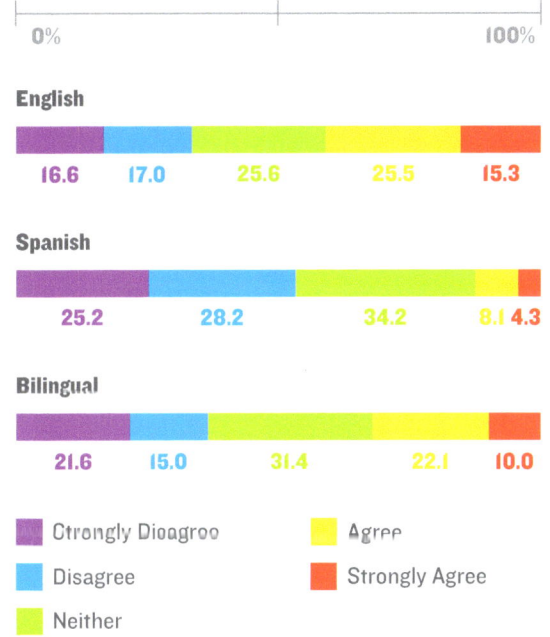

LATINO MARRIAGE & FAMILIES

Sentiments on Same-Sex Marriage

The recent Supreme Court decision making same-sex marriage legal in all fifty states has stirred up heated discussion, and most Americans have an opinion on the matter. We asked respondents for their sentiments on the following statement: "It should be legal for gays and lesbians to marry in America."

What immediately stands out (in Figure 25a) is the fact that white Americans hold far more clearly defined views of same-sex marriage than do African Americans and Latinos. The levels of indecision of the latter two groups is profound, at 43 and 35 percent, respectively. Overall approval for same-sex marriage is lowest among African Americans and highest among whites.

Support for same-sex marriage by birth cohort among the general population reveals predictable age effects (not shown). Millennials are the least likely to oppose same-sex marriage (26 percent), followed by GenXers (32 percent) and Boomers (37 percent).

Figure 25a
Level of Support for Same Sex Marriage, by Race/Ethnicity

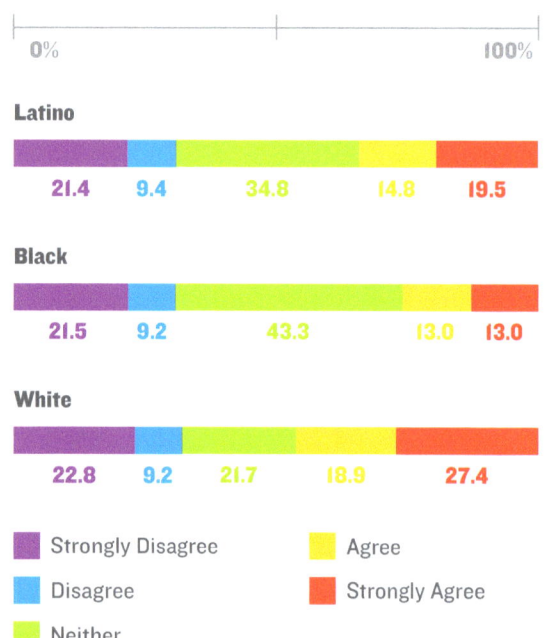

Figure 25b
Level of Support for Same Sex Marriage, by Birth Cohort (Latino only)

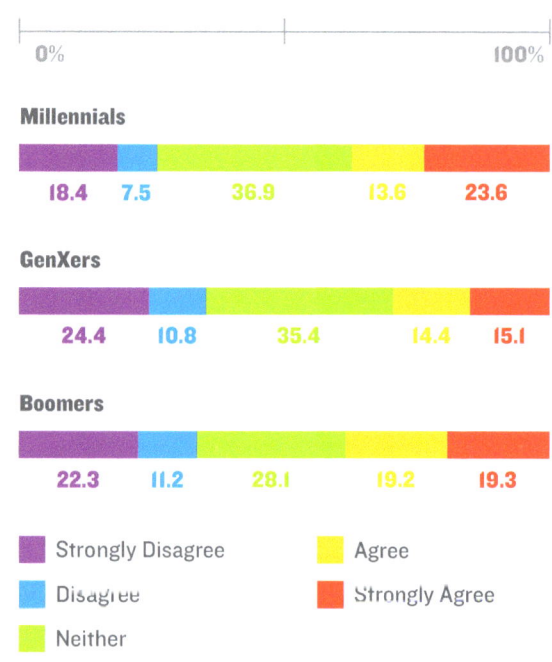

Figure 25b shows levels of support among Latinos for same-sex marriage, and these percentages look very similar to those in the general population. Just like in the United States as a whole, strong support for same-sex marriage is highest among Latino Millennials when compared to GenXers and Boomers. In terms of indifference, Latino Boomers seem to hold the most well-defined opinions on same-sex marriage, as reflected by the lower percentages who neither agree nor disagree on this question (28 percent among Latino Boomers, compared to 25 percent among Boomers overall). These findings suggest that both age effects and changes in cultural norms over time may explain support for same-sex marriage,[35] and Latinos do not differ much in this way from the general population. Millennials have grown up and been socialized in a cultural milieu that is more open to same-sex romantic relationships in general, leading to greater acceptance of nontraditional family structures. The recent legalization of same-sex marriage provides even greater cultural affirmation for the acceptance of nontraditional marriage.

Figure 25c displays results on the same-sex marriage question sorted by primary household language. Although English, Spanish, and Bilingual households show similar levels of disagreement, the percentage of Spanish-speaking households who agree with same-sex marriage is significantly lower than both English and Bilingual households. However, Spanish households seem to be characterized by the most neutral views on this question, at a commanding 44 percent, compared with 29 and 31 percent of English and Bilingual households, respectively.

Figure 25c
Level of Support for Same Sex Marriage, by Primary Household Language (Latino only)

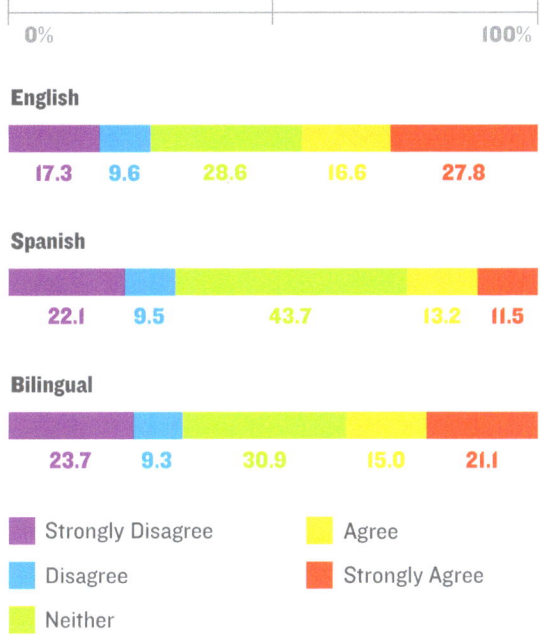

Staying Married for the Children's Sake

Children continue to be an important factor influencing marriage and marital outcomes.[36] For many couples, the decision to stay in a difficult marriage—even in the presence of persistent marital strain—is often perceived as the "least worst" option when children are involved.[37] We might expect individuals who emphasize traditional family values, and who are either Catholic or imbibe the cultural spirit of Catholicism (present in much of Latin America), to be more supportive of staying in tough marriages for the sake of children. We asked to what extent respondents agree that couples with children should stay married: "If a couple has children, they should stay married unless there is physical or emotional abuse."

Figure 26 displays the overall percentages of support for this statement. Interestingly, the highest percentage of respondents are undecided or have no opinion on the topic, followed by those who disagree. Only 28 percent agree or strongly agree with the statement. Support is stronger in the general population, then, for a couple's freedom to divorce, even if they have children and aren't in a situation of domestic abuse.

Figure 26
Level of Agreement that Couples with Children Should Stay Together

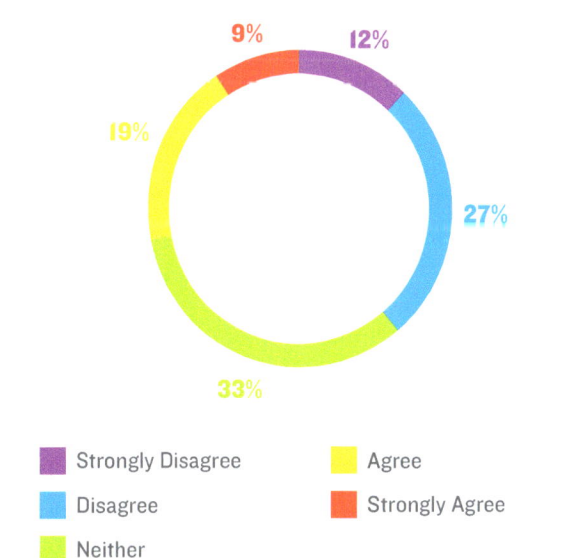

Figure 27a shows findings sorted by race/ethnicity, and they indicate that white Americans are the least traditional here. (Recall that for this question, unlike the others, disagreeing is the less traditional choice.) Latinos have the highest proportion agreeing that couples with children should remain married, at 33 percent. Indeed, one-third of Latino respondents agreed, one-third disagreed, and one-third didn't take a position on the statement. Here again, African Americans are the most "neutral" on the matter, at 40 percent.

Across generations in the population as a whole, agreement with the statement was about the same for GenXers and Boomers (26 and 28 percent; results not shown). It might come as a surprise, however, that the proportion of Millennials in agreement was slightly higher than the other two groups (30 percent). What's more, Millennials showed the lowest percentage of disagreement (34 percent), when compared to GenXers (41 percent) and Boomers (43 percent). This indicates among Boomers a greater preference for individual choice and fulfillment over marriage as an obligation. Why do Millennials appear more traditional on this question, the opposite of what might be expected? It may be that Millennials are simply more likely to feel indifferent on this matter; their undecided proportion is the largest of the three generations. Consider also that Millennials are the least likely to have experienced marriage for themselves, and they are the least likely to have already gone through a divorce. On the other hand, and perhaps most importantly, nearly every Millennial has either experienced his or her parents' divorce or knows someone who has. They may be more sensitive to the effects of divorce on children, whereas few Boomers, by comparison, have experienced this type of family upheaval.

Figure 27a

Level of Agreement that Couples with Children Should Stay Married (Unless There Is Abuse), by Race/Ethnicity

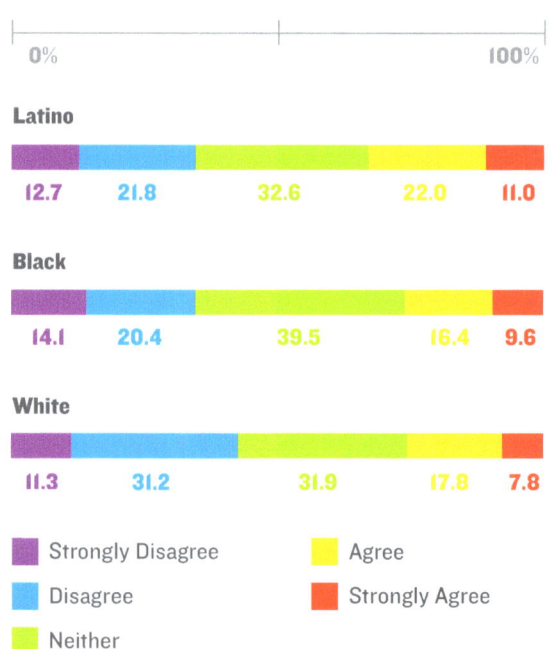

Latino: 12.7 | 21.8 | 32.6 | 22.0 | 11.0

Black: 14.1 | 20.4 | 39.5 | 16.4 | 9.6

White: 11.3 | 31.2 | 31.9 | 17.8 | 7.8

■ Strongly Disagree
■ Disagree
■ Neither
■ Agree
■ Strongly Agree

Latinos have the highest proportion agreeing that couples with children should remain married.

Figure 27b
Level of Agreement that Couples with Children Should Stay Married (Unless There Is Abuse), by Birth Cohort (Latino only)

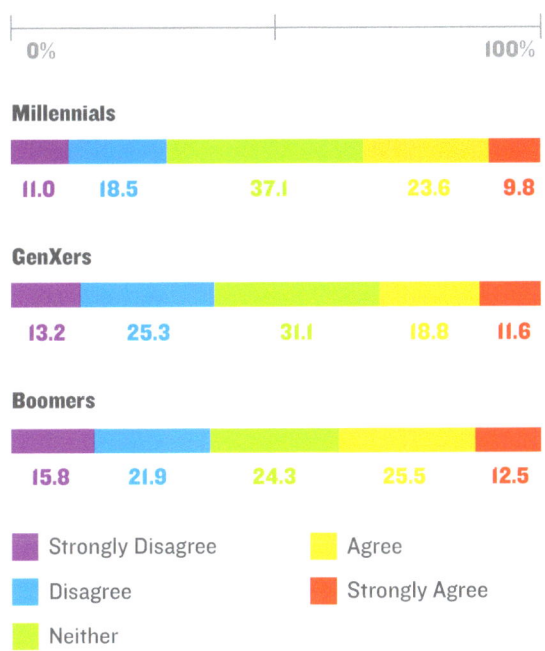

Figure 27c details that the primary language spoken in the home has little impact on views about staying married for the sake of the children. What the results from our survey suggest, however, is a high level of ambiguity. Many weren't sure what they believed was the best thing to do.

Figure 27c
Level of Agreement that Couples with Children Should Stay Married (Unless There Is Abuse), by Primary Household Language (Latino only)

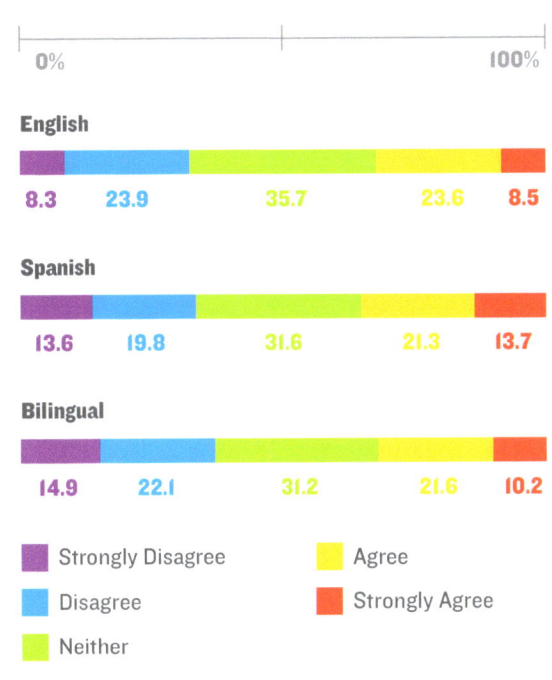

When looking at only Latinos, the findings from Figure 27b show that, again, the level of support for marital continuity varies across generations. Baby Boomers (38 percent) have the highest percentage of agreement, when compared to Millennials (33 percent) and GenXers (30 percent). As with the Americans in general, Latino Millennials appear surprisingly traditional (the least likely to disagree and only beat out in agreement by Boomers). But they are, as before, the least decided on the matter.

LATINO MARRIAGE & FAMILIES

FINDINGS FROM THE RELATIONSHIPS IN AMERICA SURVEY

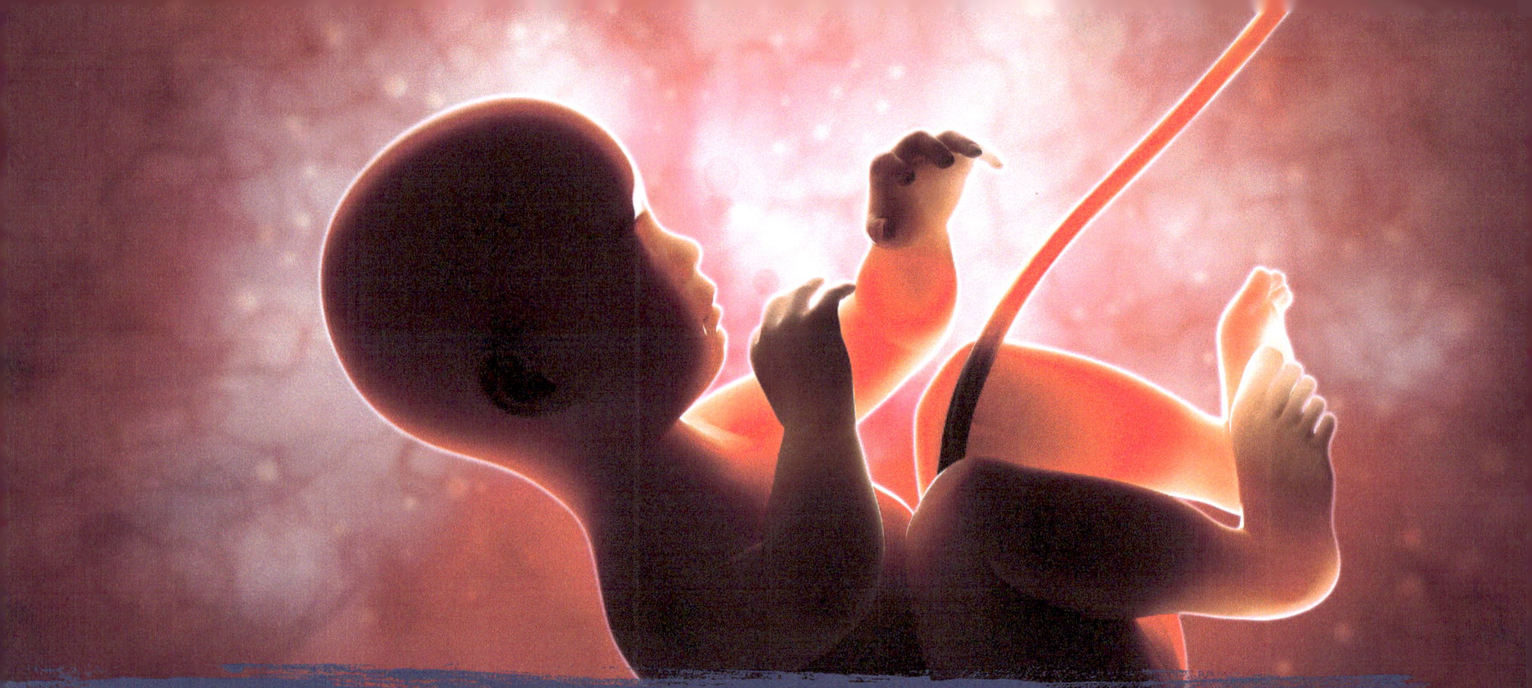

LATINOS & ABORTION

The battle between the rights of the unborn and the rights of pregnant women continues to be one of the most convoluted and polarizing arenas of public discourse in the United States. There is also considerable debate about who actually supports abortion and which side is winning over the next generation to their cause. It has been suggested that Latino Americans, who place greater emphasis on family and religion as central social institutions, must be less supportive of abortion when compared to non-Latinos.

But we must exit the charged atmosphere and look scientifically at public opinion. There is growing evidence of a shift toward pro-life attitudes among younger Americans. We assessed a level of support for abortion rights by asking for agreement or disagreement with the general statement, "I support abortion rights."

Results from our study indicate a higher percentage of respondents who either agree or strongly agree that they personally support abortion rights (39 percent). However, a sizable group of respondents holds the opposite view, as shown by the 33 percent who either disagree or strongly disagree that they personally support abortion rights.

Figure 28a sorts responses by race/ethnicity. Latinos are indeed less apt to support abortion rights than are whites and African Americans. Interestingly, African Americans stand out as having close to half of all respondents reporting indifference on the topic. Whereas 42 percent of Latinos disagreed with the statement, only 21 percent of African Americans and 33 percent of whites did so.

Table 4

Survey Response Item Measuring Support for Abortion

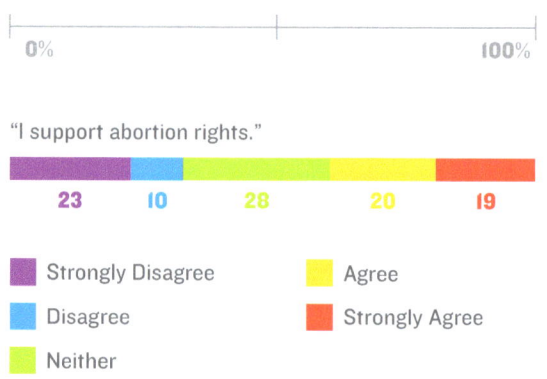

Figure 28a
"I Support Abortion Rights," by Race/Ethnicity

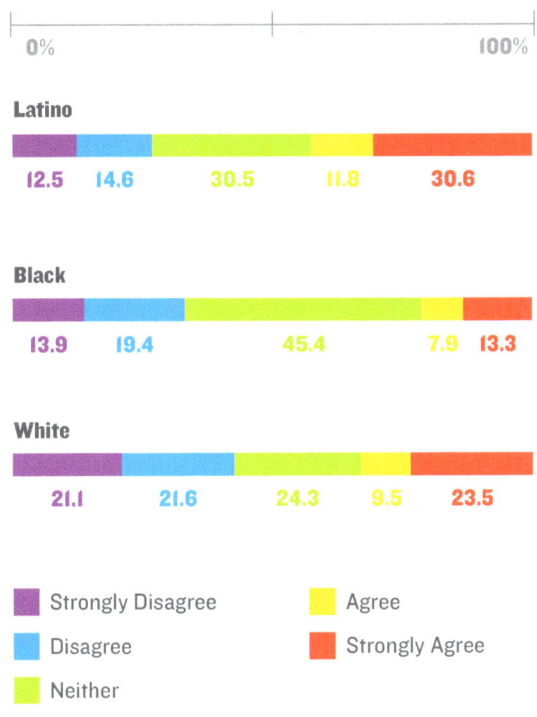

Figure 28b displays results for Latinos only, across generations. What immediately stands out is the overall lower level of support for abortion rights, as compared to the general population. What explains this? Latinos may hold stronger Catholic (and hence anti-abortion) convictions due to the traditions of their countries of origin, and they may find abortion antithetical to their emphasis on familism.

Finally, support for abortion rights is strongest (at 40 percent) in English speaking homes and weakest among residents of households where Spanish is the primary language spoken (at 15 percent). This again indicates a more traditional view of social issues in homes where Spanish is the primary language (Figure 28c).

Figure 28b
Level of Support for Abortion Rights, by Birth Cohort (Latino only)

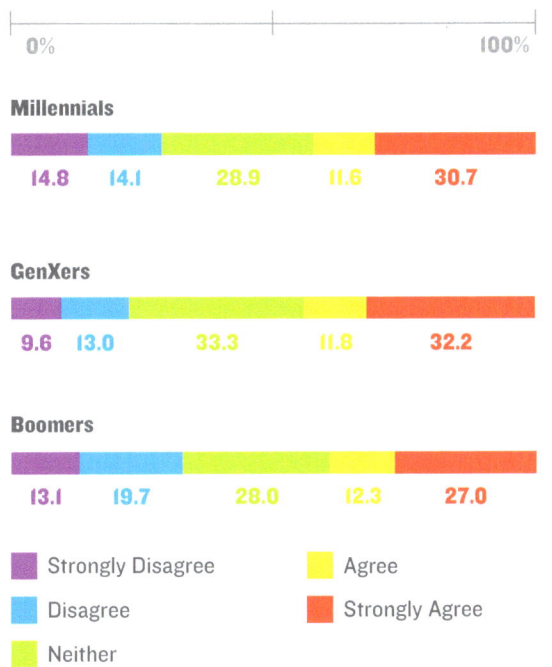

Figure 28c
Level of Support for Abortion Rights, by Primary Household Language (Latino only)

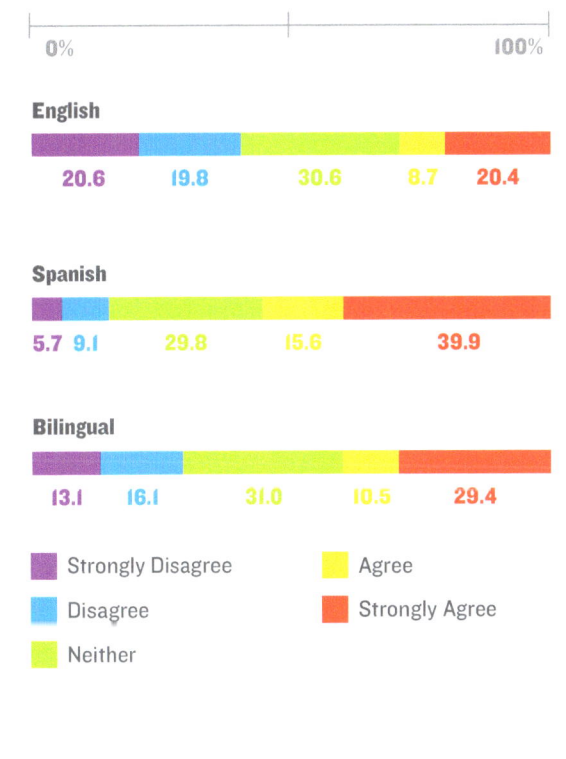

FINDINGS FROM THE RELATIONSHIPS IN AMERICA SURVEY | 37

CONCLUSION

This report attempts to shed greater light, and updated estimates, on multiple aspects of Latino public opinion using data from a large, random sample of Americans. We provide a systematic profile based on quantitative data that is removed from caricatures and preconceived notions about this growing constituency. In some areas, Latinos share views with African Americans while other beliefs are more aligned with those of their white counterparts. Still in other areas, Latinos hold distinct views that do not easily align with either group.

In general, the portrait here is one of diversity within the Latino community and not one of a monolithic constituency that aligns easily along a progressive-conservative continuum. As our findings above indicate, Latinos hold traditional values in some areas but more liberal views in others. In some instances, Latino attitudes on social issues lie somewhere between those of whites and African Americans.

It is also evident that homes where Spanish is the primary language tend generally to hold more traditional beliefs than Latino homes where English is the primary language. This suggests that Latinos who are more assimilated and have acquired greater language proficiency tend also to begin adopting more progressive views on social issues.

The report also offers insights related to the political dynamics in the Latino community. One key insight is the potential that exists within the Latino community for recruitment to either side of the political spectrum. While our data indicate a more homogeneous African American community in terms of partisan loyalty, the same cannot be said for Latinos. Latinos show both high levels of support for traditional values often associated with the Republican or conservative platform, and liberal leanings on economic issues.

Latinos are also distinct in terms of their political activism. So while Latinos may indicate less overall interest in the electoral process, this may be misleading since Latinos simultaneously indicate high levels of potential interest in becoming politically engaged. This leaves open, in our view, the possibility for mobilization.

On the other hand, Latinos also indicate preferences for more general progressive ideals, particularly in terms of economic issues. For this reason, Latinos are in a position to potentially attract "courting" from both major political parties, since the views of Latino Americans do not fit neatly into one ideological category.

We hope this report continues to add substance to discussions regarding Latino Americans and the changing demographics that could shape future political and cultural shifts in American society. The presence of two Latino candidates as potential nominees in the presidential primaries spoke to the influence of this growing minority. Furthermore, Latinos are increasingly present in positions of leadership in the media, corporate, entertainment, and political arenas. And yet, Latinos in America also face distinct economic, educational, and social challenges that will shape their political alignment and ideological views.

Recent debates over immigration, so-called "anchor babies," and growing calls for a mass deportation of millions of undocumented Latinos speaks to the complex relationship that Latinos have had historically and more recently as part of the larger framework making up American society. We see this report as an initial step in better understanding America's "majority minority" and the multidimensional character of this diverse population of Americans.

REFERENCES

Andersen, R., and T. Fetner. 2008. "Cohort differences in tolerance of homosexuality - Attitudinal change in Canada and the United States, 1981-2000." Public Opinion Quarterly 72(2):311-30.

Arland, Thornton. 1977. "Children and Marital Stability." Journal of Marriage and Family 39(3):531-40.

Axinn, W. G., and A. Thornton. 1992. "The Relationship Between Cohabitation And Divorce - Selectivity Or Causal Influence." Demography 29(3):357-74.

Baunach, Dawn Michelle. 2012. "Changing Same-Sex Marriage Attitudes in America from 1988 Through 2010." Public Opinion Quarterly 76(2):364-78.

Bumpass, L., and H. H. Lu. 2000. "Trends in cohabitation and implications for children's family contexts in the United States." Population Studies-a Journal of Demography 54(1):29-41.

Cinamon, R. G., and Y. Rich. 2002. "Gender differences in the importance of work and family roles: Implications for work-family conflict." Sex Roles 47(11-12):531-41.

DeNavas-Walt, Carmen, and Bernadette D. Proctor. 2014. Income and Poverty in the United States: 2013. Washington, DC: U.S. Census Bureau report no. P60-249. Accessed May 1, 2015 https://www.census.gov/content/dam/Census/library/publications/2014/demo/p60-249.pdf.

Desmond, M., and R. N. L. Turley. 2009. "The Role of Familism in Explaining the Hispanic-White College Application Gap." Social Problems 56(2):311-34.

Eggebeen, David J. 2005. "Cohabitation and Exchanges of Support." Social Forces 83(3):1097-110.

Emery, C. R. 2009. "Stay for the Children? Husband Violence, Marital Stability, and Children's Behavior Problems." Journal of Marriage and Family 71(4):905-16.

Ennis, Sharon R., Merasys Ríos-Vargas, and Nora G. Albert. 2011. The Hispanic Population: 2010. Washington, DC: U.S. Census Bureau report no. C2010BR-04. Accessed May 1, 2015 http://www.census.gov/prod/cen2010/briefs/c2010br-04.pdf.

Espinosa, G. 2004. "Demographic and religious changes among Hispanics in the United States." Social Compass 51(3):303-20.

Finer, L. B. 2007. "Trends in premarital sex in the United States, 1954-2003." Public Health Reports 122(1):73-78.

Freston, P. 1998. "Pentecostalism in Latin America: Characteristics and controversies." Social Compass 45(3): 335-358.

Gierveld, J. D. 2004. "Remarriage, unmarried cohabitation, living apart together: Partner relationships following bereavement or divorce." Journal of Marriage and Family 66(1):236-43.

Gooren, H. 2015. "The Growth and Development of Non-Catholic Churches in Chile." Review of Religious Research 57(2): 191-218.

Guzzo, K. B. 2014. "Trends in Cohabitation Outcomes: Compositional Changes and Engagement Among Never Married Young Adults." Journal of Marriage and Family 76(4):826-42.

Hartnett, C. S., and E. A. Parrado. 2012. "Hispanic Familism Reconsidered." Sociological Quarterly 53(4):636-53.

Hohmann-Marriott, Bryndl E., and Paul Amato. 2008. "Relationship Quality in Interethnic Marriages and Cohabitations." Social Forces 87(2):825-55.

Hossain, Z., T. Field, J. Pickens, J. Malphurs, and C. DelValle. 1997. "Fathers' caregiving in low-income African-American and Hispanic-American families." Early Development & Parenting 6(2):73-82.

Jelen, T. G. 1993. "The Political Consequences of Religious Group Attitudes." Journal of Politics 55(1):178-90.

Landale, N. S., and R. S. Oropesa. 2007. "Hispanic families: Stability and change." Annual Review of Sociology 33:381-405.

Lopez, Mark H., and D'Vera Cohn. 2011. Hispanic poverty rate highest in new supplemental census measure. Washington, DC: Pew Hispanic Center of the Pew Research Center. Retrieved from http://www.pewhispanic.org/files/2011/11/148.pdf.

Manning, Wendy D. 2004. "Children and the Stability of Cohabiting Couples." Journal of Marriage and Family 66(3):674-89.

Manning, Wendy D., Pamela J. Smock, and Debarun Majumdar. 2004. "The Relative Stability of Cohabiting and Marital Unions for Children." Population Research and Policy Review 23(2):135-59.

Motel, Seth. 2012. Statistical Portrait of Hispanics in the United States, 2010. Washington, DC: Pew Research Center, Pew Hispanic Center. Accessed May 2, 2015 http://www.pewhispanic.org/files/2012/02/Statistical-Portrait-of-Hispanics-in-the-United-States-2010_Apr-3.pdf.

Olson, D. V. A., and J. W. Carroll. 1992. "Religiously Based Politics - Religious Elites and the Public." Social Forces 70(3):765-86.

Olson, Laura R., Wendy Cadge, and James T. Harrison. 2006. "Religion and Public Opinion about Same-Sex Marriage." Social Science Quarterly 87(2):340-60.

Petersen, L. R., and G. V. Donnenwerth. 1997. "Secularization and the influence of religion on beliefs about premarital sex." Social Forces 75(3):1071-88.

Pew Research Center. 2015a. "Unauthorized Immigrants: Who they are and what the public thinks." Retrieved from http://www.pewresearch.org/key-data-points/immigration/
—. 2015b. "Hispanic population reaches record 55 million, but growth has cooled." Retrieved from http://www.pewresearch.org/fact-tank/2015/06/25/u-s-hispanic-population-growth-surge-cools/

Regnerus, M. D., D. Sikkink, and C. Smith. 1999. "Voting with the Christian right: Contextual and individual patterns of electoral influence." Social Forces 77(4):1375-401.

Sabogal, F., G. Marin, R. Oterosabogal, B. V. Marin, and E. J. Perezstable. 1987. "Hispanic Familism and Acculturation - What Changes and What Doesn't." Hispanic Journal of Behavioral Sciences 9(4):397-412.

Stark, Rodney, and Roger Finke. 2000. Acts of Faith: Explaining the Human Side of Religion. Berkeley: University of California Press.

Tach, L. M., and A. Eads. 2015. "Trends in the Economic Consequences of Marital and Cohabitation Dissolution in the United States." Demography 52(2):401-32.

Teachman, J. 2003. "Premarital sex, premarital cohabitation, and the risk of subsequent marital dissolution among women." Journal of Marriage and Family 65(2):444-55.

Vega, W. A. 1990. "Hispanic Families in the 1980s - A Decade Of Research." Journal of Marriage and the Family 52(4):1015-24.

Villarreal, R., S. A. Blozis, and K. E. Widaman. 2005. "Factorial invariance of a pan-Hispanic familism scale." Hispanic Journal of Behavioral Sciences 27(4):409-25.

Wojtkiewicz, R. A., and K. M. Donato. 1995. "Hispanic educational attainment: The effects of family background and nativity." Social Forces 74(2):559-74.

Woodberry, R. D. 2006. "The economic consequences of Pentecostal belief." Society 44(1):29-35.

ENDNOTES

1. Walter Latham Comedy, "@GeorgeLopez 'Latino in Every Home' Latin Kings of Comedy." Video post (July 22, 2012): youtu.be/yjf0IiNA5z0, accessed December 5, 2015.

2. Fox News, "Donald Trump's Immigration Plan." Transcript (August 19, 2015): tinyurl.com/hev7dzy, accessed December 5, 2015.

3. The term "institutionalized" refers to individuals who reside in correctional institutions, detention centers, mental hospitals, or nursing homes.

4. Ennis, Sharon R., Merasys Ríos-Vargas, and Nora G. Albert. 2011. *The Hispanic Population: 2010*. Washington, DC: U.S. Census Bureau report no. C2010BR-04. Accessed May 1, 2015: www.census.gov/prod/cen2010/briefs/c2010br-04.pdf.

5. Ibid.

6. These results are available in specific detail from two sources. Data on undocumented immigrants can be found in the Pew Research Center report, *Unauthorized Immigrants: Who they are and what the public thinks, 2015*. Accessed February 2, 2016: http://www.pewresearch.org/key-data-points/immigration/. Data on Latino population can be found in the Pew Research Center report, *Hispanic population reaches record 55 million, but growth has cooled, 2015*. Washington, DC: Pew Research Center, Pew Hispanic Center. Accessed February 2, 2016: http://www.pewresearch.org/fact-tank/2015/06/25/u-s-hispanic-population-growth-surge-cools/.

7. Ennis, Sharon R., Merasys Ríos-Vargas, and Nora G. Albert. 2011. *The Hispanic Population: 2010*. Washington, DC: U.S. Census Bureau report no. C2010BR-04. Accessed May 1, 2015: www.census.gov/prod/cen2010/briefs/c2010br-04.pdf.

8. Results presented in this caption are available in specific detail from two sources. Data on educational attainment can be found in the Pew Research Center report, *Pew Hispanic Center Tabulations of 2000 Census and 2010 American Community Survey. 2012. Statistical Portrait of Hispanics in the United States, 2010*. Washington, DC: Pew Research Center, Pew Hispanic Center. Accessed May 2, 2015: www.pewhispanic.org/files/2012/02/Statistical-Portrait-of-Hispanics-in-the-United-States-2010_Apr-3.pdf. Economic inequality data is found in DeNavas-Walt, Carmen, and Bernadette D. Proctor, 2014. *Income and Poverty in the United States: 2013*. Washington, DC: U.S. Census Bureau report no. P60-249. Accessed May 1, 2015: www.census.gov/content/dam/Census/library/publications/2014/demo/p60-249.pdf.

9. Correct answers: 1 (a); 2 (d); 3 (b); 4 (a).

10. Please note, the labels "Conservative Economic Values" and 'Liberal Economic Values" were not presented as part of the survey instrument when administered to respondents and are included as part of Table 2 for presentation purposes only.

11. When t-tests for different groups are compared, they show a significant difference in scores for African Americans when compared to whites (M=4.28, SD=0.07); t (15,114) =7.13, p <.001 and Hispanics (M=4.30, SD=0.06); t (15,114) =9.33, p <.001.

12. When compared to whites, t-tests show a significant difference in the scores for African Americans (M=4.47, SD=0.08); t (15,157) =8.76, p <.001 and Hispanics (M=4.43, SD=0.06); t (15,157) =10.47, p <.001.

13. When compared to whites, t-tests show a significant difference in the scores for African Americans (M=4.96, SD=0.07); t (15,155) =5.07, p <.001 and Hispanics (M=4.80, SD=0.06); t (15,155) =3.68, p <.001.

14. When compared to whites, t-tests show a significant difference in the scores for African Americans (M=4.41, SD=0.07); t (15,117) =7.58, p <.001 and Hispanics (M=4.32, SD=0.06); t (15,117) =7.32, p <.001.

15. When compared to whites, t-tests show a significant difference in the scores for African Americans (M=3.92, SD=0.07); t (15,134) = -3.33, p <.01 and Hispanics (M=3.89, SD=0.06); t (15,134) = -4.26, p <.001.

16. Jelen, T. G. 1993. "The Political Consequences of Religious Group Attitudes." Journal of Politics 55(1): 178-90.

Regnerus, M. D., D. Sikkink, and C. Smith. 1999. "Voting with the Christian right: Contextual and individual patterns of electoral influence." Social Forces 77(4):1375-401.

17. Stark, Rodney, and Roger Finke. 2000. Acts of Faith: Explaining the Human Side of Religion. Berkeley: University of California Press.

18. Espinosa, G. 2004. "Demographic and religious changes among Hispanics in the United States." Social Compass 51(3): 303-20

Woodberry, R. D. 2006. "The economic consequences of Pentecostal belief." Society 44(1): 29-35.

19. Freston, P. 1998. "Pentecostalism in Latin America: Characteristics and controversies." Social Compass 45(3): 335-358.

Gooren, H. 2015. "The Growth and Development of Non-Catholic Churches in Chile." Review of Religious Research 57(2): 191-218.

20. Landale, N. S., and R. S. Oropesa. 2007. "Hispanic families: Stability and change." Annual Review of Sociology 33: 381-405.

Vega, W. A. 1990. "Hispanic Families in the 1980s: A Decade of Research." Journal of Marriage and the Family 52(4): 1015-24.

Wojtkiewicz, R. A., and K. M. Donato. 1995. "Hispanic educational attainment: The effects of family background and nativity." Social Forces 74(2): 559-74.

21. Desmond, M., and R. N. L. Turley. 2009. "The Role of Familism in Explaining the Hispanic-White College Application Gap." Social Problems 56(2): 311-34.

Hartnett, C. S., and E. A. Parrado. 2012. "Hispanic Familism Reconsidered." Sociological Quarterly 53(4): 636-53.

Sabogal, F., G. Marin, R. Oterosabogal, B. V. Marin, and E. J. Perezstable. 1987. "Hispanic Familism and Acculturation - What Changes and What Doesn't." Hispanic Journal of Behavioral Sciences 9(4): 397-412.

Villarreal, R., S. A. Blozis, and K. E. Widaman. 2005. "Factorial invariance of a pan-Hispanic familism scale." Hispanic Journal of Behavioral Sciences 27(4): 409-25.

22. In this case, statistical tests indicate that this difference is sizeable enough that we can be confident in reporting a significant difference between Latino men and women when it comes to childhood experiences with their fathers. We carried out chi-square tests to ascertain the level of statistical significance when comparing male and female responses to these questionnaire items. The relationship between gender and attitudes towards the mother was not statistically significant at the .05 level of statistical significance c^2 (4, N = 2,334) = 22.05, p = .10. For views towards the father, chi-square was higher and statistically significant c^2 (4, N = 2,334) = 39.63, p < .01, indicating closer relationships indicating that women have closer relationships than men with their fathers.

23 Hossain, Z., T. Field, J. Pickens, J. Malphurs, and C. DelValle. 1997. "Fathers' caregiving in low-income African-American and Hispanic-American families." Early Development & Parenting 6(2): 73-82.

24. Eggebeen, David J. 2005. "Cohabitation and Exchanges of Support." Social Forces 83(3): 1097-110.

Hohmann-Marriott, Bryndl E., and Paul Amato. 2008. "Relationship Quality in Interethnic Marriages and Cohabitations." Social Forces 87(2): 825-55.

25. Sara Burrows, "Polyamory is Next, and I'm One Reason Why," Federalist (June 30, 2015): tinyurl.com/nrzxbmc, accessed December 5, 2015.

26. This question is actually more traditional than progressive, in order to reduce thoughtless answering of the questions. Answers to this question were reverse coded in order to fit the "progressive to traditional" continuum.

27. We ran analysis of variance (ANOVA) and simple OLS regression models that both indicated statistically significant differences in average scores between Latinos and the other major racial/ethnic groups shown here.

28. Analysis of variance (ANOVA) and simple OLS regression models both indicated statistically significant differences in average scores between Latinos of Mexican and Central American nationality (high traditionalism) and U.S.-born and South American Latinos (low traditionalism) on attitudes toward marriage and family.

29. Andersen, R., and T. Fetner. 2008. "Cohort differences in tolerance of homosexuality - Attitudinal change in Canada and the United States, 1981-2000." Public Opinion Quarterly 72(2): 311-30.

Olson, D. V. A., and J. W. Carroll. 1992. "Religiously Based Politics - Religious Elites and the Public." Social Forces 70(3): 765-86.

30. Analysis of variance (ANOVA) and simple OLS regression models both indicated statistically significant differences in average scores based on age. While there is no significant difference between the 18-25 and 26-29 age categories, individuals in the older categories hold more traditional categories, with all coefficients below the .05 level of statistical significance.

31. Bumpass, L., and H. H. Lu. 2000. "Trends in cohabitation and implications for children's family contexts in the United States." Population Studies: A Journal of Demography 54(1): 29-41.

Guzzo, K. B. 2014. "Trends in Cohabitation Outcomes: Compositional Changes and Engagement Among Never-Married Young Adults." Journal of Marriage and Family 76(4): 826-42.

32. Lopez, Mark H., and D'Vera Cohn. 2011. "Hispanic poverty rate highest in new supplemental census measure." Washington, DC: Pew Hispanic Center of the Pew Research Center. Retrieved from http://www.pewhispanic.org/files/2011/11/148.pdf.

33. Petersen, L. R., and G. V. Donnenwerth. 1997. "Secularization and the influence of religion on beliefs about premarital sex." Social Forces 75(3): 1071-88.

34. Finer, L. B. 2007. "Trends in premarital sex in the United States, 1954-2003." Public Health Reports 122(1): 73-78.

Teachman, J. 2003. "Premarital sex, premarital cohabitation, and the risk of subsequent marital dissolution among women." Journal of Marriage and Family 65(2): 444-55.

35. Baunach, Dawn Michelle. 2012. "Changing Same-Sex Marriage Attitudes in America from 1988 through 2010." Public Opinion Quarterly 76(2): 364-78.

36. Arland, Thornton. 1977. "Children and Marital Stability." Journal of Marriage and Family 39(3): 531-40.

Manning, Wendy D. 2004. "Children and the Stability of Cohabiting Couples." Journal of Marriage and Family 66(3): 674-89.

Manning, Wendy D., Pamela J. Smock, and Debarun Majumdar. 2004. "The Relative Stability of Cohabiting and Marital Unions for Children." Population Research and Policy Review 23(2): 135-59.

37. Emery, C. R. 2009. "Stay for the Children? Husband Violence, Marital Stability, and Children's Behavior Problems." Journal of Marriage and Family 71(4): 905-16.

APPENDIX

The data in this report are part of the larger RIA project. RIA is a nationally representative probability sample of 15,738 non-institutionalized adults between the ages of 18 and 60 residing in the United States. The survey was fielded in January and February 2014 by GfK Group, formerly known as Knowledge Networks, a company with a strong record of generating high quality, nationally representative surveys.

GfK recruited the first online research panel that is representative of the entire U.S. population. Panel members were randomly recruited through probability-based sampling, and households are provided with access to the Internet and hardware if needed.

GfK recruits panel members by using address-based sampling methods (formerly GfK relied on random-digit dialing methods). Once household members are recruited for the panel and assigned to a study sample, they are notified by email for survey-taking, or panelists can visit their online member page for survey-taking (instead of being contacted by telephone or postal mail). This allows surveys to be fielded quickly and economically. In addition, this approach reduces the burden placed on respondents, since email notification is less intrusive than telephone calls, and most respondents find answering internet questionnaires more interesting and engaging than being questioned by a telephone interviewer. Furthermore, respondents have the freedom to choose what time of day to complete their assigned survey.

RIA was conducted in both English and Spanish. Of those contacted, 62 percent completed the survey. To increase completion rates, GfK contacted potential respondents three and six days after the survey was fielded to remind them to complete the survey.

In order to correct for biases that may be introduced by non-response, GfK provides survey weights so that each sample is representative of the nation as a whole. Appropriate survey weights were used in every estimate in this report, unless otherwise indicated.

In each of the questions asked in the survey, some small fraction of respondents refused to answer the question, or skipped the question. Skip/refusal rates were generally quite low for most questions, and although slightly elevated for other questions, were still quite low for even sensitive questions. Questions about abortion were outliers, often garnering refusal rates above 10 percent. Most questions exhibited lower than five percent refusals or skips. Such cases were eliminated from analyses of items for which they skipped or refused to answer, unless otherwise indicated.

www.ingramcontent.com/pod-product-compliance
Lightning Source LLC
Chambersburg PA
CBHW060809090426
42736CB00003B/211